The Gard...
DOM

Polly Pattullo and Anne Jno Baptiste

Illustrations by Nancy Osler
Cover painting by Marie Frederick

The Papillote Press

Very many thanks to:
All the gardeners and farmers of Dominica featured in this book
who showed us around their gardens and were so generous with
their time and knowledge

We are also indebted to:
Dennis Adams, Cuthbert Jno Baptiste, Valerie Bloom,
Eileen Burton, Margaret Busby, Lennox Honychurch,
Patricia Honychurch, Ros O'Brien, Ashworth Simon,
Caroline Whitefoord and Val Wilmer. And to Roger Hird,
Liz McCabe, Peter Luscombe, Eddie Thomas and the Guardian
newspaper systems department for technical support

A CIP catalogue record for this book is available from the British
Library
ISBN: 0 9532224 0 3

The Papillote Press
Published in the United Kingdom
23 Rozel Road, London SW4 OEY
Printed by Ace Duplicating Services, Parmiter Street, London E2 9HZ

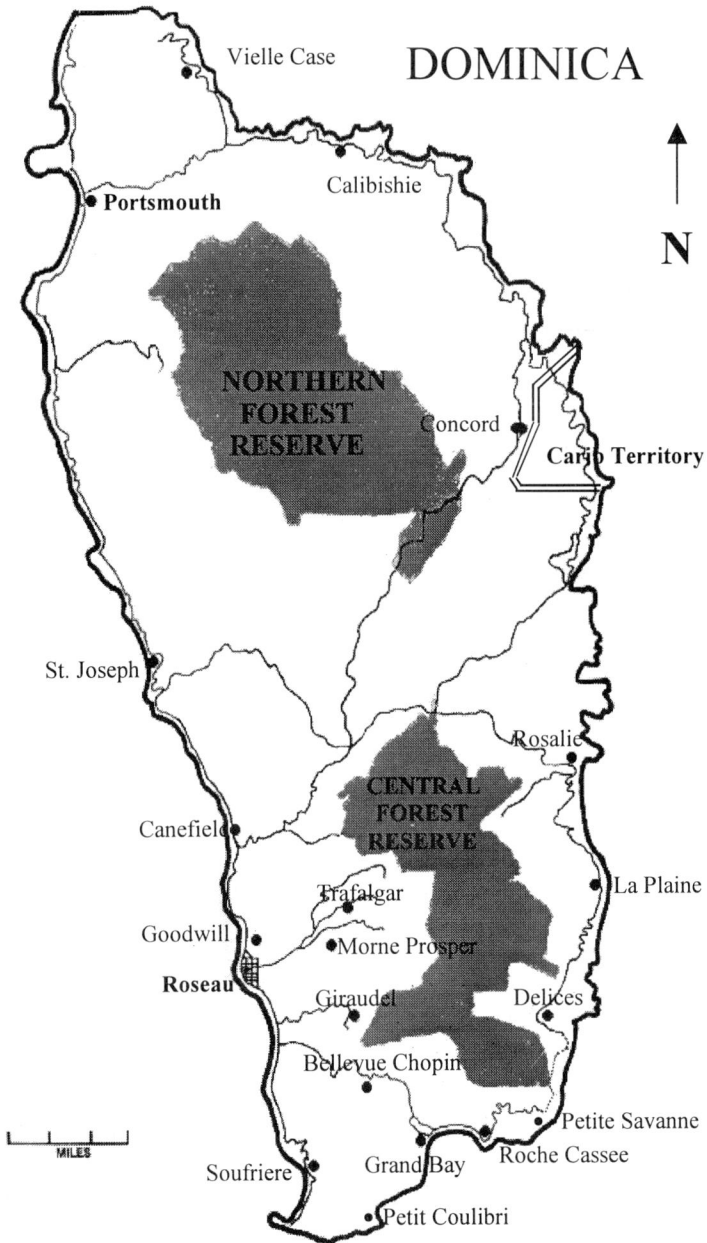

DOMINICA

N ↑

Vielle Case

Calibishie

• Portsmouth

NORTHERN FOREST RESERVE

Concord •

Carib Territory

St. Joseph

Rosalie

CENTRAL FOREST RESERVE

Canefield •

La Plaine

Trafalgar

Goodwill •

• Morne Prosper

Roseau

Giraudel

Delices

Bellevue Chopin

MILES

Petite Savanne

Roche Cassee

Soufriere

Grand Bay

• Petit Coulibri

Contents

INTRODUCTION

A ll Dominica is a garden. And Roseau market – every Saturday morning – is a celebration of the island's gardens, a display of the bounty of fertile valleys and mountain ridges.

The market sellers – mainly women – arrive before first light, set up their tables or find space on the ground. Their produce is neatly displayed in 'heaps': red hot peppers beside green cucumbers, rosy pink grapefruit and the angular yellow carambola keep company with breadfruit, green bananas and mighty piles of hairy yam and tannia, the ubiquitous 'ground provisions' of the Caribbean. Then there are armfuls of agapanthus and day lilies, delicate posies of white daisies and pom-pom dahlias, and buckets of ginger lilies. Watermelons and jelly coconuts are sold from the back of trucks; there are tomatoes and mangoes; watercress in damp baskets; herbs tied in slender bunches with 'banana rope', and bouquets of medicinal herbs for bush teas.

All this is an expression of Dominica's climate and topography and of the industry of its people (after all, the national motto is *Après Bondie C'est La Ter*: After God it is the Earth). Most of the market produce is grown by smallholders, peasant farmers who cultivate an

Nutmeg.   Bougainvillea.   Lemon Grass.   Castor Oil

immense variety of crops on one or two-acre pieces of land. The market also illustrates how the encounters with all those who reached Dominica's shores have shaped its traditions of cultivation: Amerindian Caribs, European planters and African slaves, each brought their own. Most recently, another group, the Taiwanese, has introduced Chinese vegetables into the local horticultural inventory.

The drama of Dominica's landscape – its great north-south spine of rainforested mountains, high ridges and deep valleys – means that each corner of the island has a mini-climate of its own, with its own indigenous plants and particular conditions for cultivation. Gardening at a high altitude on volcanic soil in the interior, for example, offers a different experience to managing a coastal garden on limestone deposits. Mango, sugar cane and coconuts flourish on the coast, for example, but do less well at high altitudes; similarly, temperate plants, at home in high places, shrivel and die at the coast. The Atlantic winds of the windward side also create conditions that contrast to the gentler breezes, 15 miles away, on the west coast.

The windward side and the hinterland receive the most rain – up to 300 inches in the interior – while rainfall in parts of the hotter west coast, lying in the rain shadow, totals less than 50 inches. The volcanic soil is richest in the coastal valleys. Crops and flowers burst into growth in the year-round 'summer', constrained only by the most destructive of storms or the testiest of droughts.

How does your garden grow?
In Dominica, a garden is not just the 'tamed' area around the house. It describes any piece of cultivated land. When Dominicans say, 'I going to my garden' they may mean that they are going to 'weed up' their newly planted ginger lilies near the house; they may also mean that they are going to tend their bananas, to pick avocados or to plant their provisions (root vegetables). Their 'garden' may be around their back door or many miles from their house. So gardens are never simply good to look at, they don't just have a decorative function: they produce and provide in a variety of ways – for food, trade, medicine, religion as well as for pleasure. Indeed, gardens are an integral part of Dominican lifestyle and culture – for almost everyone is a landholder of some sort and a grower of some thing.

Dominica's first gardeners were the Amerindians who arrived in Dominica from South America in various waves of migration through

Ginger Lily. Agapanthus. Aloe Vera. Coffee. Oxalis

the Lesser Antilles. The Caribs were the last Amerindian group to arrive, probably around 1250 AD. It was the Caribs who fought the first European adventurers, and it is only in Dominica (and St Vincent) that they survive as a people. Botanists believe that there were few edible plants in the native vegetation of the Lesser Antilles. What is likely is that the Caribs (and their predecessors), who settled around the mouths of Dominica's many rivers, brought with them from South America many of the fruits and vegetables that the Europeans found when they first arrived in the Caribbean.

For five centuries, European explorers, missionaries, anthropologists and botanists have noted (sometimes inaccurately) the practices of Carib agriculture. When the Europeans first reached Dominica they saw that the Caribs grew cassava, corn and sweet potato and cultivated fruits such as soursop, papaya, guava and pineapple. All these and more – larouma (a reed used in basketwork) and arrowroot, for example – are probably native to mainland south America. Soon after the first encounter in 1493, plants introduced from Europe, such as bananas and sugar cane, and then breadfruit and mango were to be found in the 'jardin caribe'. The first borrowings or plant cross-overs from one culture to another – a process which is at the heart of Creole culture – had begun.

But it was always a sustainable mixture, whether of native or introduced species – and remains so today. As the Dominican historian Lennox Honychurch writes: 'Today, more than ever, the subsistence agriculture of the jardin caribe provides an assurance of food supply and nutritional stability which the fluctuating cash income of the neo-plantation economy of the banana industry cannot.'

Modest French estate houses

The first Europeans to settle in Dominica arrived at the end of the 17th century. Rough-hewn French adventurers rather than refined grandees, they cleared land for lumber, grew a little cotton and tobacco (crops of the new world) and exported root crops to Martinique. Their gardens would have reflected a struggle for survival rather than pleasure.

In any case, despite the acceleration of colonial expansion, there were never grand estate houses in Dominica, such as those in Barbados or Jamaica whose surrounding gardens reflected European fashion, with formal gardens of fountains and parterres. The land was too challenging for mass clearing of the forests for plantations. Extant

Datura. Mango. Bwa Kwaib. Chinese Hat. Gardenia

Dominican estate houses suggest something far more modest. An 18th-century painting by the Italian artist Agostino Brunias, for example, of a settler's house in the Roseau valley shows the immediate landscape around the house and the adjacent slave quarters. The painting is illustrated in the book, *The Dominica Story* by Lennox Honychurch, who captioned the painting as follows: 'Plantains ripen on a frame, while balizier, castor oil, logwood and cocoa plants flower along the river banks.'

Coffee was the first major plantation crop in Dominica, introduced soon after 1725 by the French, who had estates in the south, around Soufriere, and also in the north. Much later, the British, who colonised the large coastal valleys, concentrated on sugar, sometimes alternating with coffee and cocoa. The demand for sugar in Europe encouraged Dominican planters to increase sugar production, and with the need for more labour, more African slaves were brought to Dominica.

After emancipation, sugar production declined, although coffee and cocoa continued intermittently, to be replaced by limes at the end of the 19th century. For a time Dominica was the world's largest producer of limes, but then disease and changing economies decimated the industry. Now, the only evidence left of the neat orchard estates once owned by L.Rose & Co is a glimpse of the crumbling stone terraces around Soufriere. Since the 1950s, bananas have replaced limes and now underpin the Dominican economy.

During the years of the plantation system, while the estates dominated the lower, more fertile areas, the slaves were allowed to make their own 'provision grounds' on the steep slopes of the foothills. Unlike some other Caribbean islands, there was plenty of land available in Dominica. In any case, it made economic sense for the estates to allow the slaves to feed themselves. European visitors reported, usually but not always in defence of slavery, that the slaves cultivated 'great quantities' of root crops, tobacco, okra, corn, beans and fruits for their own consumption or to sell in the local market on Sundays.

Noting the entrepreneurial skills of the slaves, the French naturalist F.R. Tussa wrote: 'The yam is an important commercial subject for the free Negroes and the slaves, who cultivate them in their gardens, sell them at the markets found on Sundays.' An Englishwoman called Mrs Carmichael, the author of a remarkable book entitled *Domestic Manners and Social Conditions of the White, Coloured and Negro*

Cacao. Amaryllis. Vanilla Frangens. Spathiphyllum

Population of the West Indies, observed (in Jamaica) that 'The fruit
trees upon an estate are, by common consent, the prerequisite of the
negroes belonging to it. The West Indian islands differ as to their
productiveness in fruit, but generally speaking, there is a great variety
of fruits, according to their season; and upon every property the
negroes make a considerable sum by the sale of their fruit.'

Whatever the political and economic relationship between Caribs
and Africans and Europeans, there would have been exchanges of
plants and seeds, customs and practices between the groups. By the
18th century, for example, the slaves – and the Europeans – were
using the indigenous hot capsicums of the Caribs, while the Caribs
and Europeans were growing yam and okra, which had been
introduced from West Africa.

Although not writing about Dominica, it is worth noting that Mrs
Carmichael comments that she gave seeds, brought from England, to
'her labourers', of cabbages, turnips, carrots and peas. Likewise, the
slaves would have exchanged cuttings and seedlings for their
provision grounds, with memory triumphant over the Middle Passage
in a continuity of African traditions. In Roseau market, the practice of
placing fruit and vegetables in small 'heaps' (the word is still used:
'how much a heap?') echoes West African market custom.

Maroons, Caribs and slaves – the art of subsistence farming
By the end of the 18th century, runaway slaves, known as maroons,
had established communities in many parts of the island, surviving by
subsistence farming in their own remote forest 'gardens'. In the 1780s,
when the conflicts between the maroons and the British were at their
height, British governors noted that the maroons were finding
sustenance from the *wa wa,* the wild, indigenous yam. And that
tradition of subsistence peasant gardening, practised by the maroons in
the mountains, the Caribs in their *jardins caribe* and the slaves in their
provision grounds, has continued to the present day. In a sense, the
following description (if somewhat sentimental) of peasant production
in the village of Laudat, high above the Roseau valley, in 1900 could
have been written either before the end of slavery or, indeed, even
now at the end of the 20th century. 'A little garden patch, some goats,
a few beans, yams, bananas, and other tropical fruits for the picking,
their every want was supplied,' wrote an American visitor to
Dominica. Until the 1960s, travellers from the east coast passed

Veti-ver. Kaka Poul. Balizier. Yam. Crape Myrtle

through Laudat on their way to and from Roseau; now it is better known to visitors as the setting-off point for hikes to the Boiling Lake.

A great plant melting-pot

When Europeans arrived in the Caribbean, they realised that many plants that grew in other parts of the world would flourish in the Caribbean. Even temperate plants would grow in high elevations, while Mediterranean species, such as jasmine and pomegranate, which arrived with the first Spanish settlers, would grow almost anywhere. The date palm, ginger, citrus, melon and cucumber, and, via the Canaries, banana and sugar cane, took root in those early years.

Plant species also arrived from West Africa. By the early 1700s, many varieties of African yam, guinea grass, castor oil, black-eyed peas, pigeon peas, peanuts and okra had reached the Caribbean on slave ships. Yam, in particular, was a staple African food (hence the word *nyam,* which means to eat in Caribbean English, while the Dominican Creole word for yam is *igname*), and became ubiquitous during slavery. A Danish botanist and anti-slavery campaigner, Paul Erdman Isert, who accompanied a slave ship from the coast of Guinea to present-day St Croix in 1788, observed that the food given to the slaves on board ship 'consisted for the most part of products from their own land, such as maize, rice and yams. They seemed to find our pearl barley very tasty.'

So by the end of the 18th century, species upon species had reached Dominica in particular and the Caribbean in general – from Britain, Italy, Spain, China, Mexico, India, the East Indies, Africa and the Pacific.

In the early days, the arrival of plants in Dominica was probably somewhat haphazard, depending on the economic interests and fancy of planters and traders. Such 'immigrants' came on slave ships or in the holds of warships or sloops, or were taken as booty from enemy ships. Logwood, for example, once a valuable timber, arrived in the Lesser Antilles in the early seventeenth century, plundered by pirates off ships sailing from the Yucatan to Europe. While the mango, indigenous to the East Indies, was first taken to Jamaica from a French ship bound for Hispaniola by the British fleet of Lord Rodney in 1782.

However, by that time, the dispersal of plants had become more organised, especially when Sir Joseph Banks, the President of the Royal Society in London, initiated the setting up of a network of bot-

Topitambour. Croton. Pride of Barbados. Coralita

anical gardens in the British colonies. Behind all this extraordinary movement of plants lay a great imperial design – to enrich the far-flung colonies and thereby make the British Empire even greater. But if there was self-interest, there was also scientific and intellectual purpose in improving the quality and management of plant life in all the colonies.

A key development took place in St Vincent, to the south of Dominica, where the first botanical garden in the new world was set up in 1765. The transfer of plants from the East Indies to the West Indies thus became systematic rather than haphazard. Around the same time, the Society of Arts in London offered prizes to planters in the West Indies to experiment in the cultivation of cinnamon. At this period, too, ideas about the environment, the relationship between forest cover and rainfall were also being discussed; this was important given the tracts of land being cleared for sugar in the Caribbean.

Some of the plant arrivals to Dominica at this period came, not surprisingly, from St Vincent's Botanical Gardens, where, most famously, the breadfruit had first arrived in the new world in 1793. Its migration, from Tahiti, was part of a grand plan, orchestrated by Banks. He had taken up the request of a Jamaican planter to provide a new food for slaves, 'which would have the great advantage of being raised with infinitely less labour then the plantain, and not subject to danger from excessively strong winds'. Captain Bligh was appointed captain for the voyage from Tahiti to the Caribbean with a British naval ship given over to breadfruit plants, under the supervision of two gardeners. And at his second attempt (the mutiny on the Bounty occurred on his first voyage), Bligh accomplished his task.

Three hundred breadfruit seedlings and 'other useful and curious plants' were left in St Vincent, in the care of the great Scottish-born curator of the Gardens, Alexander Anderson. Of these, some made their way to Dominica. A letter from the manager to the absentee owner of the Wallhouse estate, near Loubiere in Dominica, in 1800, records the progress of two breadfruit plants. 'The two breadfruit at Wallhouse are alive,' was the curt comment.

Banks, who was so instrumental in bringing the breadfruit to the Caribbean, never went to the region, but plenty of other plant-hunters did. Records suggest that, although they set off for home with their own treasure pots of specimens, they also left plants in the islands. Exchanges of plants, among Caribbean planters themselves, also facil-

Caladium. Logwood. Grapefruit. Hibiscus. Bean

itated the dispersal of old world plants among the islands of the new. There is a detailed account, for example, by a French coffee planter called William Urban Buée of the first clove tree (a native of the Moluccas) to arrive in Dominica.

In 1789, Buée received a six-inch-high clove tree 'having six to eight leaves' from a friend in Cayenne, the capital of the French colony (now French Guyana) on the South American mainland. Buée planted his fragile clove seedling 'with great care' between four of his coffee trees on his Montpellier estate, in the Roseau valley. After six months, the seedling had failed to put on any growth, so two more plants were sent from Cayenne. This time Buée planted them near his house, on different, red-clay soil: 'they grew fast and with luxuriance', and in six years his trees were bearing fruit. More seedlings were bought in Martinique. Buée hoped to make a killing, but it was not to be. In the end, he was ruined by Britain's protectionist policies.

Despite Monsieur Buée's failed venture, visitors to Dominica at the end of the 18th century reported favourably on the fertility of the land and how bountifully everything grew. Alexander Anderson, on a brief plant-hunting visit from St Vincent, said that of all the Windward Islands, Dominica's vegetable 'kingdom' was 'by far superior'. Thomas Atwood, whose book, *A History of the Island of Dominica*, was published in 1791, described how Dominica 'produced many species of fruit peculiar to the West Indies; all of which grow there in great perfection'. He also listed innumerable vegetables and herbs, many of temperate origin; again, reported Atwood, in Dominica they grew to 'great perfection'.

Two doctors link up with Kew Gardens

Later, two other Europeans were to make distinctive contributions to the island's agricultural development. Both were British medical doctors, exemplars of Victorian vigour and scholarship. For much of the 19th century, Dominica languished in poverty and colonial neglect, but this did not deter Dr John Imray, who arrived in Dominica in 1832. Imray became famous for his research on the causes of and cures for tropical diseases, notably yellow fever and malaria, but he was also a well-versed botanist, who discovered new species of flora in Dominica. Significantly, it was Imray who also introduced Liberian coffee, a hardier variety of tobacco via Kew Gardens and the lime (his estate at Batalie was described as 'a forest of lime trees') to Dominica.

Zeb Mal Tet. Banana. Oleander. Coconut. Cassava

In 1873, another doctor, H.A.A. Nicholls, arrived on the island. Nicholls took over Imray's other remarkable estate, at St Aroment, above the present-day suburb of Goodwill. There, Nicholls busied himself with the propagation and model cultivation of hosts of tropical plant species, notably limes and coffee. He described many of his experiences at St Aroment in his book *The Textbook of Tropical Agriculture* (1892), which was to become a standard work.

Nicholls was also at the forefront of botanical experimentation and in close touch with the Royal Botanical Gardens at Kew, which described him as 'the indefatigable correspondent of Kew in Dominica'. In 1890, for instance, Nicholls wrote to Kew: 'I have succeeded in flowering the Chinese Ginger at Saint Aroment, and I send you a botanical specimen (taken from a shoot fully 4 and a half feet high) by this mail. You will be enabled from this specimen to determine the plant, and I hope I may be the first in the field. I was really the first to get the Yoruba indigo to flower, but foolishly I did not send on specimens to Kew. I have other specimens of Chinese Ginger flowers pressing, and you can have them if you wish.' Nicholls also sent specimens of the island's indigenous plants to Kew while, in exchange, Kew sent him plant material. In the 1887-88 Kew Bulletin, Nicholls listed an incredible 99 'economic plants' from all over the world then growing in Dominica. The article also noted that 30 species of palm grew at St Aroment.

The establishment of Dominica's Botanical Gardens in 1891 – first stocked in part from St Aroment – provided another channel for the introduction of new plants. It was one of several established in the Caribbean at that time (although more than a century later than the one in St Vincent) as part of a colonial strategy to develop island economies and improve the standards of agricultural practice. By then, Dominica was concentrating on sugar, cacao, limes, and coffee.

In 1902, F. Sterns-Fadelle, a Dominican planter, wrote a pamphlet called *Dominica: A Fertile Island*. It was an attempt to attract investors to Dominica, but it faced up to the economic problems suffered by the island. Fadelle mentioned aspects of island life of which Dominica could be proud. Of the botanical station, he wrote: 'By furnishing well prepared plants to all parts of the country, it has largely contributed to the extensions of the cultivation of cacao, limes, fruits and spices throughout Dominica, where it is a self-supporting institution, and an interesting depository of large and choice varieties

Dasheen. Mamey Apple. Trumpet Vine. Raspberry

of vegetable specimens, useful and ornamental.' While the Botanical Gardens concentrated on agricultural plants, and an agricultural school was established above the Gardens at Morne Bruce (where the cabbages were, according to Fadelle, 'quite equal to importations from New York and much cheaper'), there were also the private gardens – in town or around the estates – of the white and emerging 'coloured' elite. They now had access to dramatic flowering plants, 'exotics' such as bougainvillea, which arrived in the Caribbean in the 19th century, as well as the long list of earlier arrivals. European-style gardeners enjoyed re-creating rose-strewn flowerbeds mixed with the more flamboyant flowering shrubs.

Less popular perhaps, but more appropriate for Dominica was to integrate indigenous plants into these 'new' gardens. This, for example, is how the writer Jean Rhys remembered her grandparents' estate house at Geneva in the south of the island at the end of the 19th century. 'The steps down to the lawn. The iron railings covered with jasmine and stephanotis. In the sunniest part of the garden grew the roses and the 'English flowers'. But in the shadow the Sensitive Plant which shuts its leaves and pretended to die when you touched it, only opening again when you were well away. The gold ferns and the silver, not tall like tree ferns but small and familiar. Gold ferns green and cool on the outside but with gold underneath which left an imprint if you slapped a frond on your hand.'

This lovely, evocative piece of writing illustrates how in Dominica it is impossible to separate what is and what is not 'cultivated'. The ferns of Geneva earned their place as much as the roses. It is hard to contain the 'bush' and, in any case, the glory of many Dominican gardens depends on integrating the 'wild' and the 'cultivated'.

Herbs for bush teas in every yard

There are plants, for example, all around Dominican homes, which are not always formally cultivated, yet they are not 'weeded up' and remain a fundamental ingredient of every garden. These are plants used medicinally, according to the practices of folk medicine. During slavery, herbal remedies were used both to prevent and cure disease, while herbs were also a component in obeah. Atwood, at the end of the 18th century, acidly mentioned that obeah practitioners were 'generally well acquainted with the quality of many poisonous herbs that grow in the West Indies.'

Fromager. Petit Manioc. Pea. Glyricidia. Beetroot

The knowledge – and use – of herbal remedies remains with both Caribs and Afro-Dominicans despite an increased dependence on formal Western medicine. A study of Dominica's medicinal plants in 1988 identified 62 plants used in a wide range of complaints, from piles to bed-wetting to high blood pressure. Plants are sometimes used in baths and poultices, while bush teas, from a variety of plants found around the home, are commonplace; nowadays they are also sold in tea bags. Some of the most common medicinal plants, both indigenous and 'imported', that are seen in Dominican yards include periwinkle (*Kaka poul*), lemon grass, wild sage (*Lantana camara*), kudjuruk (*Petiveria alliaceae*) and wormweed (*Simen contra*).

The great period of migration of plants to the Caribbean is now over, but every day new plants probably still arrive in Dominica as Dominicans return from nearby Guadeloupe or faraway London or Toronto. In some cases, the introduction of new plants can be traced to particular individuals at a particular date.

Red anthurium and purple impatiens

The magnificent spears of the torch ginger (*Nicolaia elatior*), for example, were first introduced to Dominica by an American businessman called Leo Narodny, who brought samples of the plant from Puerto Rico in the early 1940s. The red ginger lily (*Alpinia purpurata*), now popular as a cut flower, was introduced only in the early 1960s when a young English architect working on the original Fort Young Hotel brought these plants, native to Indonesia and the Pacific, from Trinidad. Similarly, the startling agapanthus, with its big ball-of-blue bloom, was brought to Dominica by the late Clem Dupigny, owner of the Ridgefield Estate, also in the 1960s.

While the pink anthurium has long been grown in shady places, the hybrid red anthurium was not seen in Dominica until the 1970s when Pete Brand, the American owner of the former Island House Hotel (destroyed by Hurricane David in 1979) in Wotten Waven, imported some plants from Hawaii. Now, both the red and pink – as well as many other hybrids from Holland, France and Hawaii – are bought by the armful from market sellers. The hot pinks, orange and purple impatiens, now seen both in gardens and as escapees carpeting damp wild places, can also be traced back to Brand.

Another influential figure was the late Alan Pugh, a Welsh expatriate. Pugh distributed cuttings of the green and white *Dracaena*

Soursop. Cordyline Terminalis. Azalea. Cush-cush

sanderiana, commonly known as Lucky Lily, for villagers to grow. He then collected the grown plants as cut foliage to be shipped to England on the Geest banana boat. Nowadays, *Dracaena* is commonplace along roadsides, particularly in the Carib Territory.

These relatively new arrivals have been quickly assimilated into Dominican gardens, with new plants generating new ventures. As in other aspects of Dominican culture, there has been borrowing and assimilation from one tradition to another in response to economics and fashion. One Dominican remembers a bed of the pale blue *Plumbago capensis* and deep red shrub roses in a villager's garden in Calibishie, on the north coast, in the 1930s: plants that had at some stage moved from the estate's garden to the estate worker's garden.

At the same time, the Dominican peasant has usually had to put survival first, hence the useful breadfruit, hot peppers, banana, dasheen and papaw in every yard, rather than the sharp colours of the decorative bougainvillea. The ethnobotanist W.H. Hodge reported on a journey from Roseau to Bellevue Chopin in 1944. Travelling along the 'shore road', he noted that 'seaside hovels' were 'made picturesque' by 'the ever present breadfruit or mango tree'. Poverty and living circumstances precluded the establishment of the sort of flower gardens enjoyed by the bourgeoisie. According to one Dominican, who grew up in the 1950s in Pointe Michel (a west coast village through which Hodge would have passed): 'People would grow flowers in their yards, but then somebody's goats would come and eat them, or chickens would scratch them up. So villagers would give up on flowers. But there would always be plants around, not consciously cultivated but just as part of everyday life.'

There is also the long established tradition of *koudmen* (helping hand) in which the community gathers around to help a neighbour with a major chore such as building a house or clearing a garden. In this project, the men do the cutlassing, clearing and digging, the women weed, plant and provide the meal, while the children fetch the water. The division of labour around the yard would have traditionally seen the women tending and planting, with the men handling the hoe and pickaxe. This is now a less common division of roles: for women head many households and many women are farmers.

Roseau market would not always have been so full of the diversity of produce as exists today. In times of economic depression, hardship or bad weather, when the land would not produce and the people had

Sea Grape. Tamarind. Cannonball Tree. Tannia

no money to spend, the economic conditions would be reflected in the market produce. In 1954, James Pope-Hennessy, an English diplomat and writer, found little to admire about Roseau's appearance. Of the market he said, 'the poverty of the market of Roseau has to be experienced to be believed.' He described, '...a sad lilliputian display of country produce spread out upon the dusty ground, while would-be purchasers squawk and giggle and gossip and quarrel over two mangoes, four sweet potatoes, one christofine or a handful of chickpeas.'

New houses sprouting new gardens

In a generation, the improvement in the standard of living and the emergence of a cash economy has generated the plentiful produce now seen in Roseau market. That economic shift has also given a greater emphasis to the 'beautifying' of homes and yards, and to the decoration of churches every Sunday and for festivals. And when the terrible hurricanes of 1979 destroyed every blade of grass, every tree, everyone had to start again from scratch – it was a useful social equaliser. Aid programmes in the wake of Hurricane David introduced many new varieties of lettuce, beets and cabbage, while schools cultivate gardens both to teach children about plants and to be conscious of their environment.

Across all classes and groups, there is now a new interest in gardening. New planting techniques have given impetus to flower gardening on a grander scale, while the advent of cable television has stimulated new ideas for gardens and flower arrangements (with titles of entries in flower-arranging competitions sometimes taken from American soap operas). This process has been accelerated by the expansion of new housing, belonging both to wealthier Dominicans (including retirees who have returned from abroad, with ideas gleaned from the United Kingdom or Canada) and to lower-income groups.

New houses sprout new gardens from Grand Bay to Marigot. It is a great leap from older attitudes which perceived the landscape in purely functional, God-given terms. Dominica's claim to be the 'Nature Island of the Caribbean' – if it's not to be an empty piece of propaganda – means the protection of the rainforests and reefs, of sustainability, of growing good things without chemicals, of respecting the natural order. A contribution to this has been made by Rastafarians, who emphasise the 'natural'. The threats to Dominica,

Jacaranda. Bauhinia Purpurea. Tobacco. Kalanchoe

like to other parts of the world, centre on an unqualified admiration for what is in fashion. Uniformity in Dominican gardens would be a kind of betrayal of the island's biodiversity.

Gardens, like plants, bloom and fade, and there are gardens in Dominica now invisible, long pounded by sun and rain, and then swallowed up and reclaimed by the invasive green forest. One such was Mount Joy, an estate on the Imperial Road. In the early 1930s, an English wanderer and artist called Stephen Hawys established a home there. He described his first view of the garden in his book of his days in Dominica, *Mount Joy*. 'It had once had a very beautiful small garden, and among the overgrown bush one could see occasional roses of good family – aristocrats which had known better days. There were allamandas, like golden cups upon incredibly long stems which had been fighting the love-vine and the guava bushes for years to win a place in the sun, and jasmine too...The field immediately below the terraced garden, edged with congested thickets of iris, waved with sugar-cane, and beyond that was a tangle of untutored guavas...I could hardly see anything from the house door for a huge pink hibiscus tree the colour of mange on a white dog, and a glyricidia, covered with wisteria-like mauve flowers, filled the foreground.'

At Mount Joy, Hawys created an important garden, nurtured his roses and became an authority on orange growing and mangosteens. With his death in 1968, the forest reclaimed his garden and now, if you tread carefully around the land that was once his, you might find a gnarled old citrus that has survived both his coming and his going.

That is the nature – indeed the story – of Dominica's gardens. But this book looks backwards only in its attempt to explain. More importantly, it is concerned with the present – with the diversity of the gardens of Dominica and the need to protect and cherish them. We have chosen to celebrate the great gardening culture of Dominica by featuring – in the broadest sense – those gardens which illustrate different traditions and locations: by the sea, in the mountains and forests, in villages and towns.

The gardens that we feature are by no means the only delightful gardens in Dominica. Each village, each section of roadside where people live or work all have gardens to appreciate and enjoy. For to peer into any garden in Dominica is to uncover the story of how people – whether Carib, African or European – at every point in Dominican history have planted a 'slip' in the soil and watched it grow.

'All Dominica is a garden'

Eye-catching potted plants of ferns and
flowering shrubs adorn a small Roseau home

ROSEAU

While there are signs of a growing awareness in Dominica about the value of the old and the historic, this has come too late for many of the town houses – and gardens – of Roseau. Much of the capital's Victorian architecture, houses with gingerbread fretwork and wooden verandahs overhanging the street, has been either badly neglected or torn down for new commercial buildings.

There is little evidence left of the courtyard gardens that once graced the capital's older, wealthier homes. Houses were pulled down when middle-class families moved out to the suburbs. In a few cases, the houses remain, but the gardens have gone, with only a glimpse of papaya or breadfruit straining for light between the new buildings; or a hardy, ancient mango tree has been spared when homes expanded into courtyards to accommodate growing families. Sometimes you can see, beyond stone walls, the remnants of stables and outhouses, a glimpse of cobblestones and a patch of grass. Or behind a gate, an elderly lady struggles to maintain a garden of potted orchids and ferns.

Historically, the richer residents of Roseau, snug behind their high walls from the poverty of the streets, treasured their sweet-smelling shrubs such as honeysuckle, tended their small-bloomed roses for cut flowers, enjoyed an array of herbs and other pot plants on the verandah and made sure of a mango or avocado tree. One Dominican fondly remembers his grandmother's house and garden in King George V Street (now the site of the Liat airline office), which had a grape vine, jasmine climbing around the wrought-iron gate, a pond and fountain, a little bed of lettuce, chives and thyme for the kitchen.

Kingsland House, also on King George V Street, is another lost Roseau town garden. Pulled down in the 1960s and now the site of Astaphan's general store, it had been the town residence of the agriculturist H.A.A. Nicholls and his family at the turn of the century.

By the time the English writer Alec Waugh paid a visit to Dominica in the 1930s, Nicholls was dead and Kingsland House had been turned into a guesthouse, run by Nicholls' daughter, Maggie. Waugh described Kingsland House in his book, *The Sugar Islands,* and remembered it as a peaceful resting-place. Describing the gardens, he wrote: 'Mangoes were ripening; the plants bordering the lawn were

Granadilla. Baby's Breath. Watercress. Peperomia

studded with blue blossom; the tulip tree was still in flower, its bright
red mellowing to orange; beyond the convent a poui tree whose
presence before I left I had not suspected was now a brilliant splash of
canary yellow against the deep green of the Morne; a hen was
shepherding four infant ducks beneath the bay tree...'

Kingsland House was also where Dr Nicholls had had his famous
conservatory for his orchids. The conservatory was immortalised in
the novel, *The Orchid House,* written by his writer/politician grand-
daughter, Phyllis Shand Allfrey. In the novel, Allfrey remembers,
through the voice of Lally, the family nurse, how the Old Master (Dr
Nicholls) 'would stand there under that roof of palms plaited with
bamboos, unhanging wire baskets to dip his plants into a tank
swarming with tiny fish: the fish were there to eat mosquito grubs.
Very often he got paid for his attention with rare flowering things; the
poor patients knew his hobby. He would scoop out bits of log and fill
the hollows with charcoal, then bind these queer roots with coconut
fibre. Hours and hours he would spend there making beautiful labels,
and goodness the number of names one spray might have, written in
his small script: Cattaleya crispa purpurea – Bee orchid or golden
shower – Madonna or Eucharist or Holy Ghost orchid...'

Apart from those much-loved private homes and gardens, the
public buildings of colonial Roseau were also dressed for the
occasion: State House, the home of the administrator, had large and
splendid grounds. The library, built in 1905, the gift of Andrew
Carnegie, was likewise surrounded by well-tended gardens and
fountains. The bishop's house and adjacent Catholic cathedral both
had gardens that reflected the prestige of the institution.

In contrast to the buildings of the political and religious
establishment and the homes of the elite, the rest of Roseau, during
colonial times, was largely blighted by poverty and neglect. Even so,
Frederick Ober who visited Dominica in the 1870s found it 'green
with fruit-trees, and over broken roofs and garden walls of roughest
masonry hang many strange fruits. Conspicuous are the mango,
orange, lime, pawpaw, plantain, banana and tamarind. Over all the
town the cocoa palms, their long leaves quivering, their dense clusters
of gold-green nuts drooping with their weight.'

A rather less lyrical view came from James Pope-Hennessy, in the
1950s, who found much to dislike about the colonial mentality of
Dominica – and the appearance of Roseau. And in his book *The Baths*

Broccoli. Lettuce. Frangipani. Bois Canon. Bamboo

of Absolam, he wrote: 'From the verandah [of the La Paz guesthouse where Whitchurch, the supermarket, now stands] to the other side of this lane I could gaze over a chequerboard of rusty tin roofs and untidy backyards. It was a world of scratching, scrawny hens, and charcoal stoves, of crouching silhouettes and greasy cooking.'

Much of that overt poverty has now disappeared from the streets of Roseau. Greater wealth and the devastation wrought by Hurricane David have brought new, concrete office blocks – but also the disappearance of Ober's town that was 'green with fruit trees'. Even so there are still small corners of eye-catching greenery in Roseau: pot plants crammed beside stone steps spill over on to the street from the tiniest yard while rows of plants flourish in old paint tins, rubber tyres, plastic tubs or whatever container is at hand.

And there remains a handful of homes with lovingly tended front gardens. One of these is outside the family home of Reginald Winston. This pretty, white wooden house is on Great Marlborough Street, just round the corner from the Banque Française. Its tiny garden is tucked between the verandah, which itself is full of ferns and window boxes of impatiens, the elegant curves of the front steps, a few inches of lawn (is it cut with nail scissors?) and a low wall which separates the private space from the public street. No corner is wasted and the garden spills over on to the street where the delicate pale blue blossoms of plumbago form a hedge under the wall. And even beyond, there is garden: a strip of grass has been planted at the edge of the pavement.

Reginald Winston, a lawyer in government service, is an enthusiastic gardener who gets up early each morning to plan and tend. He gets ideas from other gardens when he travels or finds inspiration from sitting on the wall and thinking. There are roses and yellow shrimp plants (*Acanthaceae beloperone guttata*) behind the garden wall, while two Norfolk pines and three intertwined bougainvillea give height to the garden. Along a side wall there is a thriving bignonia vine, brought from Barbados, and close by, a collection of orchids, hanging in bamboo containers.

In such a confined space, there is always pruning to be done, especially of the larger specimens, and daily watering of the many potted plants. One of the constraints of this town garden is that because of its orientation, for much of the year there is full sun only for a few hours in the morning; as a result window-box plants such

Pitcairnia Angustifolia. Cinnamon. Tweff. Piment

as geraniums are restricted to the sunnier months. What is particularly effective is that the garden complements the house but does not submerge it.

Reginald Winston doesn't know why so many tourists stop and take photographs of his family's house and garden when, as he says, there are so many beautiful gardens elsewhere in the world. The answer may be that Roseau has so few remaining gardens that the one at the Winston house on Great Marlborough Street is a delightful rarity in its robust defiance of modern trends.

A plan to control the encroaching concrete is being developed by the government as part of a project to restore the old French section of Roseau (close by the old market place). The Dominica Conservation Association and the Dominica Association of Architects have drawn up a proposal for a pedestrian walkway and a periphery road to link Roseau and its famous Botanical Gardens in a way that would emphasise the town's historical features. With the renewed appreciation of old buildings must come a belated pride in protecting the remaining old town gardens.

The Botanical Gardens

The Botanical Gardens lie on a gently undulating site, about half a mile inland from Roseau's Bay Front. Once known as the best in the Caribbean, the Gardens may no longer be able to justify such a reputation but they remain a cool, peaceful corner, connected to but separate from the bustle of Roseau.

The Gardens were first planned, on a 40-acre site, in 1891 by the London officials of the Royal Botanical Gardens, Kew. The Gardens' main function was to be 'strictly of an experimental and economic character'; they were for work, not for play. The Kew Bulletin for 1891 reported, following a visit by one of its officials, that: 'ornamental plants are to be grown in moderate quantities for rendering the grounds attractive and interesting, but chief attention will, it is hoped, be devoted to the plants of an economic or industrial character, and especially those likely to be in demand for establishing new plantations in Dominica'.

Only after this objective had been achieved was there to be a secondary use for the Gardens: 'As the land is larger than is absolutely required for the nurseries, beds, and experimental plots of a Botanical

Pumpkin. Sweet Corn. Job's Tears. Bwa Cotelette

Station,' reported the Bulletin, 'it may be desirable to lay down such parts as are not immediately required in grass, and plant it with shade and ornamental trees'.

To carry out their mission, the Gardens' pioneering plantsmen, Charles Murray from Edinburgh's Botanical Gardens and, most famously, the long-serving superintendent of Roseau's Botanical Gardens, Joseph Jones, brought plants from all over the world to Dominica. Dr Nicholls also supplied cuttings, seeds, bulbs and seedlings from his St Aroment estate, outside Roseau.

The Gardener's Chronicle of 1893 described how the newly opened Botanical Gardens had been laid out in plots for 'economic plants' – these included Liberian and Arabian coffee, different kinds of cacao, cinnamon, limes, Chinese ginger, oranges, tangerines and mulberries. The walkways between the plots were 'lined with pineapples of various kinds, Egyptian cotton, nutmegs and other ornamental plants.' By the end of the century, the reputation of Dominica's Botanical Gardens had been established. And it was earning glowing reports. By then, Mr Jones could also report healthy plant sales of limes, oranges, cacao, coffee, nutmegs and cloves.

Attention had also been paid to the ornamental side of the Gardens. The planter, F. Sterns-Fadelle, who belonged to Dominica's 'coloured elite', wrote in 1902 of what he called 'the fine People's Park' adjacent to the botanic station. 'The good taste displayed in its arrangement, and the scrupulous care bestowed on it, render this suburban resort a most attractive one, and our diligent Curator has in this respect also deserved well of all lovers of the picturesque. It is not vast, like the prater of Vienna, nor gorgeously ornate, like Battersea Park, but ours is indisputably the most charming recreation ground in the West Indies, not excepting the beautiful tended gardens of Georgetown, Demerara.'

In their heyday, before the second world war, the Gardens were famed throughout the Caribbean, and boasted more than 500 species of exotic and indigenous trees and shrubs. Over the years, economic constraints and then the destruction by Hurricane David in 1979, which reduced the Gardens to a 'junkyard of tree limbs', have taken some of the gloss off the Gardens' reputation. However, even the reduced numbers of species has not seriously diminished the pleasure of wandering around the Gardens, watching cricket (in one of the best settings in the world) or sitting in the shade of a stately tree.

Blue Petrea. Flamboyant. Periwinkle. Bee Orchid

The Gardens were once famous for their palms, including a great avenue of wine palms. Many were destroyed but some remain, as do a large number of other non-indigenous trees that you may not see elsewhere in Dominica. Among them are a cannon ball tree (*Couroupita guianensis*) with its sweet-smelling flower and foul-smelling fruit, from South America; the African baobab (*Adansonia digitata*), which squashed a yellow school bus in Hurricane David, and a spectacular fig tree (*Ficus banjamina*). The Gardens also grow Dominica's national flower, known locally as Bwa kwaib (*Sabinea carinalis*). This small deciduous tree, with scarlet flowers, is endemic to parts of the dry, leeward coast of Dominica.

The economic section of the Gardens, which is where its story began, remains an important feature. The Gardens is the headquarters of the Forestry Division of the Ministry of Agriculture. Close by is the government laboratory responsible for testing water and soil, the vet's office and offices of regional agricultural research organisations. An aviary for breeding Dominica's two endangered indigenous parrots, the Imperial (Sisserou) and the Red-necked (Jacquot), is adjacent to the nursery, which sells seedlings to farmers, thus continuing the role advocated by the colonial pioneers a century ago.

What to look out for A classic tropical botanical gardens, mixing indigenous trees with species from every corner of the world. A map of the Gardens is available from the office of the Forestry Division, based in the Gardens, during office hours.

How to get there Enter from the Bath Road or Valley Road.

What else to see in Roseau

State House Opposite Fort Young Hotel, originally the home of the colonial administrator, now used for state and public occasions. Its lawns and trees remain, although the description by J.A. Froude, the arch-imperialist, who visited Dominica in the 1880s, suggests that it had a more exciting garden then that it has today (hurricane damage has not helped). 'The house was handsome, the gardens well kept; a broad walk led up to the door, a hedge of lime trees closely clipt on one side of it, on the other a lawn with orange trees, oleanders, and hibiscus, palms of all varieties and almond trees, which in Dominica grow into giants, their broad leaves turning crimson before they fall,

Citronelle. Ficus. Sausage Tree. Pak Choi. Lemon

like the Virginia creeper. We reached the entrance of the house by wide stone steps, where countless lizards were lazily basking. Through the bars of the railings on each side of them there were intertwined the runners of the largest and most powerfully scented stephanotis which I have ever seen.'

The Bishop's House, Turkey Lane. Neat lawns set off the pretty white building set back from the road. Some parts of the garden are planted with pink oleanders. There is also a row of old mango trees. Nowadays, the garden is neat, tidy but not particularly noteworthy.

The World of Food, Queen Mary's Street. This was the childhood home of the Dominican-born writer Jean Rhys. Much of the original interior of the house has been lost, but a great mango tree survives in the courtyard (now a bar/restaurant). This old tree featured in a chapter in Rhys' unfinished autobiography, *Smile Please.* 'Where are you going?'[asks her nurse] 'Into the Garden. I walked out of the sun into the shadow of the big mango tree.'

Fort Young Hotel, next to the public library and opposite State House. Once the area of the old fort, it then became police barracks, when it was set out, according to the turn-of-the-century book *In Old Roseau,* to flowers, shrubs, coconuts, limes, lemons and Smyrna figs. Now there is some attractive planting of ornamentals around the bar area and on the terrace facing the sea.

Cherry Lodge Guesthouse, Kennedy Avenue, has a narrow little flower bed beside the open-sided eating area. It has an old Roseau atmosphere (the guesthouse was called Cherry Lodge after its cherry tree – now long gone), and is planted with Eucharist lilies and the spiky, red-bloomed indigenous bromeliad, *Pitcairnia angustifolia.*

Bath Road Note the miraculous survival of a night-blooming cereus cactus by Eve's Photo, just south of the government headquarters.

Window boxes and hanging baskets. Outside some restaurants.

Style of the suburbs

Better-off Dominican families now tend to live in the suburbs outside Roseau rather than in the city centre. As a result, areas such as Canefield and Goodwill (to the north of Roseau), Elmshall and Bath Estate in the Roseau valley, and Castle Comfort (to the south) have developed. Residential homes now colonise the slopes of ex-sugar

Samaan Tree. Campeche. Century Palm. Larouma

estates, where the air is cooler and the atmosphere more peaceful.

Goodwill, with St Aroment on its upper reaches, is a dry, sunny area facing the sea and the sunset. As you climb the hill, the houses of the professional classes become larger and more luxurious and the gardens expansive, dominated by lawns and shrubs, such as bougainvillea and multi-coloured crotons. The houses have a Californian-ranch style – with garage space for two or more cars and large parking bays; swimming pools are still rare.

One of the nicest and most ably planted gardens belongs to Dr and Mrs Green who live in St Aroment. The garden that surrounds the Greens' house on one acre of sloping land shows the rewards of creativity and hard work, effectively using the hot, sunny and dry conditions. Part of the old sugar estate, this young garden, cleared from bush in 1991 but with some old trees retained, has gradually matured and shows the passion of its owner for cut flowers.

Above the house, the garden is edged with young palm trees on one side and the arching mauve-flowered branches of the crape myrtle shrub on the other. Around the steps to the house is a selection of different-coloured hibiscus while, under a wall, stand the handsome iris-like neomarica, some mauve and some yellow. Towards the back of the house is a row of pink and red ginger lilies and below them a selection of hybrid heliconias. Both these plants produce dramatic blooms used for flower arrangements, along with the anthurium in shady areas. The garden shows a flair for colour and design using familiar tropical flowering shrubs.

Opposite the Greens' house lies the former St Aroment estate, its buildings now dismal ruins, its gardens lost in green confusion. Once it was different. As the Royal Gardens Kew Bulletin, for January 1891 reported: 'In the afternoon a visit was paid…to the St Aroment Estate, where cacao, lime trees, Liberian coffee, and numerous interesting plants have been carefully cultivated for many years, first, by the late Dr Imray, and now by Dr Nicholls, F.L.S. This place is one of the most interesting spots in the Leeward Islands.'

What to look out for Suburban-style gardens with lawns, bougainvillea, hibiscus, allamanda, and cut flower species.

How to get there For Goodwill, cross the Roseau River going north, go straight on and turn up Federation Drive at the roundabout.

Zingiber Officinale. Guinea Poivre. Manjack. Mibi

Republic of China Agricultural Mission

The Republic of China has had a mission in Dominica – just outside Roseau at Stock Farm – since the mid 1980s. Its function is to offer technical help to the Ministry of Agriculture with its diversification and planning programmes. 'Our main objectives are to help farmers produce more effectively and to develop crops for export,' said Yin-Chuen Ma, former head of a seven-strong team at the mission.

A 'super sweetcorn', a Taiwanese hybrid, is one of the many new crops recently introduced by the Taiwanese. This sweetcorn (the local variety is basic maize) harvests in 65 days and is now being exported to Antigua and St Croix. It requires intensive care in planting and maintenance and needs pesticides. But the quality and yields are high, and the ripening is uniform, said Chief Ma. The mission is concentrating on the drier Salisbury and Layou Valley area for this crop, offering seedlings free of charge, to enthusiastic farmers.

The Taiwanese have also introduced farmers to a new variety of papaya. This small tree produces very sweet fruit, and takes nine months to harvest from transplanting. Each tree deteriorates after bearing fruit for one season. The Taiwanese also recommend the use of pesticides for this fruit crop. Among other crops introduced by the Taiwanese are broccoli and cauliflower, Chinese cabbage, long white radish, asparagus, string beans and the cherry tomato.

What to look out for A Chinese demonstration farm with plantings of fruit (including the miniature papaya tree) and vegetables.
How to get there North of Roseau, turn right after Egbert Charles building suppliers, follow road up the hill. Telephone:44-84250

Shipwreck Cottages, Canefield

This is a very pleasant seaside garden, where the tree-planting offers shade from the hot sun of the small beach. Although this garden was not consciously designed, it has developed during its 17 years of existence into a mature landscaped area, dominated by palms.

Part of an old sugar, then lime and banana estate, it had only two mango trees and two sea almonds in a bleak, brown landscape when its owner, Patrick James, first saw it. Now the palms (royal palms near the house, bottle, date and coconut palm, and a cluster of arengas and

Strelitzia Reginae. Hog Plum. Fat Pork. Thunbergia

latania) create a set of narrow vistas through to the sea. The coconut is the most economically valuable of the palms. Thought to have originally come from the Pacific Rim, the coconut was well established in the Caribbean by the 17th century, and has long been used as a food and drink, for oil and soap, the husks for coir and the back bones of the leaves for brooms. Coconut estates are most common on the north coast of Dominica.

Like many other Dominican gardens, Shipwreck is probably most colourful in May and June when the yellow and red flamboyants and the Pride of Barbados are in flower. There are also three frangipani, a pink, a yellow, and a white. Some cacti, collected from the even drier west coast area around Colihaut, are clustered around and on a rock. There is further use of dry planting with agave and pineapple.

Patrick James has dug a well, which enables him to water and he plans to develop more water plants. He already has an old teche (copper sugar pan) filled with the pale lavender-blue water hyacinth. This hyacinth also flourishes on the sand. Cleverly irrigated with piped water, the garden is even beginning to burgeon on the beach.

What to look out for Palms and cacti on the edge of a beach

How to get there On the road from Roseau to Canefield, take the left-hand road at the turning for the industrial estate, then carry on to the sea. Telephone: 44-91134.

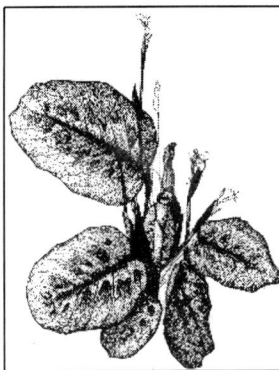

ROSEAU VALLEY

This is a majestic area stretching inland from the town of Roseau. It encompasses the villages of Trafalgar, Fond Cani and Wotten Waven in the fertile Roseau River valley, while along the arms of the old volcanic craters sit the villages of Morne Prosper on the southern ridge and Laudat, high up on a parallel ridge to the north. Lime trees once filled the most fertile, flatter lands of the lower Roseau valley helping to make Dominica the world's largest producer of limes. The British company L. Rose & Co presided over the production of limes on the island for nearly a century until the industry's final demise at the turn of the 1980s. Photographs of the Roseau valley earlier this century show acres of neatly organised rows of lime trees filling the flat lands of the valley. At the turn of the century, Dominica produced nearly 30,000 tons of limes a year. Raw and concentrated lime juice was shipped abroad in barrels. Essential oil could also be extracted from the lime skin by moving the fruit by hand over a spiky tool which collected the oil at its base. But now the lime industry is history in the valley.

Although there is some new interest in tourism, the villages of this area close to Roseau, with their high rainfall and good volcanic soil, remain highly productive. Most villagers are farmers cultivating their small 'gardens' of perhaps a couple of acres. Morne Prosper, for example, grows three-quarters of all the thyme exported from Dominica to neighbouring Caribbean islands.

These four gardens in the Roseau valley illustrate the diversity of this richly endowed area of Dominica: a typical small market garden; a larger smallholding specialising in peppers; an internationally-regarded garden of bromeliads, aroids, begonias, gingers, heliconias and orchids, and a delightful estate garden where you can see tropical fruits and vegetables growing along specially designed trails.

Solandra Nitida. Bay. Philodendron Giganteum. Dill

Papillote Wilderness Retreat Gardens

These four acres of nurtured wilderness lie at the head of the Roseau River valley, just below the Trafalgar Falls. Carved out of the rocky slopes, the garden, with its guesthouse and restaurant, nestles in a canopy of tree fern and breadfruit. This provides a green frame for the many 'mini-environments' of this rainforest garden created by Anne Jno Baptiste, the co-author of this book. There are intensive collections of begonias and bromeliads, aroids, heliconia, gingers and indigenous orchids planted in family groups and in settings, which set off shape, colour and texture to best advantage. 'They blend from nurtured collections into wilderness,' says Anne Jno Baptiste. And to the casual observer it just might all be natural, such is the sense of luxuriance and tangled growth. Yet it has been designed with great care and to great effect. The trails, which criss-cross hot and cold mineral water streams and wind across the contours, lead from one themed glade to another. It's also a haven for bird and animal life.

Papillote is the second incarnation of a garden that Anne Jno Baptiste first started in 1967 – with a collection of ferns, mosses and orchids. This garden was destroyed in 1979 by Hurricane David when the whole valley, stripped of its soil and vegetation, turned from lush green to brown and bare stone in a few hours. But there was an end to the destruction: tree ferns, papaw and pumpkin seedlings were the first post-hurricane signs of life.

The high rainfall (around 200 inches a year), the rocky soil and the altitude (1000ft) mean that the Papillote garden reflects its mini-climate. It constrains the gardener, but it enriches the content of the garden by demanding a homogeneous and coherent style. Constant attention has to be paid to terracing, drainage systems and erosion control, and to mulching, to build up the soil, while support systems, such as old tree stumps, are never discarded. They have become a second home for bromeliads and orchids. Similarly, the stone animal statues dotted around the garden have acquired their own special collections of mosses and fern.

Anne Jno Baptiste is committed to conserving indigenous species – and she has rare aroids, such as the *Philodendron giganteum* and *Anthurium dominicense*, collected long ago from the rainforest, in addition to the endangered orchid, *Epidendrum discoidale*. She also experiments with exogenous species, keeping in touch with internat-

Sorrel. Mimosa Pudica. Bottle Brush Tree. Parsley

ional developments, exchanging seeds and plant material with specialists overseas, and sending for unusual seeds, such as the surreal *Amorphophallus paeoniifolius.* This is closely related to the giant *Amorphophallus titanum,* which drew crowds of admirers to London's Kew Gardens when it flowered for the first time in July 1996. Papillote's close relation flowered in June 1997. The aquamarine jade vine is another extraordinary plant that flowers at Papillote between January and May, spreading its leaves on an overhanging orange tree.

Papillote's display of endemic and imported bromeliads is a garden in itself, with the terrestrial bromeliads planted among the epiphytes, which perch snugly on sections of tree fern. Among the collection is *Nidularium innocentii* 'Viridis' with its carmine-tipped lime green leaf; close by is another *Nidularium,* the 'black Amazon birdnest', with rusty orange showy bracts. Close by are the well-established arching stems of the indigenous *Pitcairnia angustifolia,* which are often also found on roadside cliffs.

The name of the garden dates from the early 1850s, the post-emancipation years. According to the written testimony of an elderly villager in the nearby village of Trafalgar, '...after slavery was over the master told his slaves to go out and build there [sic] house far out, they do, there was two of them go down to that land was Pappi and Alliotte.' So this was no large estate, but the land of peasant subsistence farmers, the sort of people who for so long have been the backbone of the Dominican economy. The remnants from that era can be seen in the proliferation of breadfruit, papaw, cacao and citrus.

Papillote today has a different style, which within a green wilderness, incorporates its history, the changes fashioned during its more recent past and its ever-maturing present.

What to look out for A rainforest garden, with an international reputation, in a wilderness. Look for the collections of begonias, heliconias, aroids, bromeliads, indigenous orchids, gingers and ferns. A new map has been compiled for visitors so that they can identify plants as they wander the trail; spot the animal statues or take a dip in the natural hot pools. A garden tour costs EC$5. Restaurant and accommodation available.

How to get there Go to the end of the road past Trafalgar village to the junction before the Trafalgar Falls. Telephone: 44-82287

Watermelon. Rose. Surinam Cherry. Cassia Fistula

D'Auchamps Estate, Trafalgar

This lovely nine-acre estate was part of the original Shawford estate, centred further down the Roseau valley with its mill and water wheel. After sugar cane, the estate produced coffee and then citrus; and it was abandoned citrus fields that the Honychurch family found when they moved to D'Auchamps in 1979. At first they developed it as a private garden pulling out old citrus trees to make lawns, but since 1994 garden trails have been created to form delightful walkways through natural dry forest leading into plantings of fruit trees, flowering shrubs and vegetables typical of Dominica.

The trails have an educational purpose: 'I am trying to develop the sections to show the different plants that visitors would see on the shelves in their local supermarkets as ready-to-buy fruit and vegetables and demonstrate how they are grown here,' says Sara Honychurch, who trained as a landscape designer. She has plans to develop an interpretation centre which will show the history of plant production in Dominica.

The trail begins beside a wide lawn backed by different spice trees, and moves through dramatic plantings of heliconia and pink gingers with pink anthuriums massed on the bank in the shade of forest trees. There are spectacular viewing spots over the Roseau valley and across to the peaks of Morne Watt and Morne Anglais. The trail continues through a shady area of large trees, including the dramatic African tulip tree *(Spathodea campanulata)* whose bright red flowers bloom from December to March, before opening out into the 'village garden' section: here are rows of dasheen, sweet potato and yam, all popular ground provisions, and the vine of the christophene, a pale-green, pear-shaped member of the squash family. Close by is Captain Bligh's corner, the man responsible for bringing the breadfruit and its relative, the breadnut, to the West Indies. Wild raspberries (*Rubus rosaeifolius*) called *fwaize,* also flourish.

On a wonderfully open grassy slope is an orchard planted with endless varieties of citrus, guava, mamey apples, soursop, Barbados cherry and so on. Crush a citrus leaf and you can smell the tang of tangerine or orange, grapefruit or lime. Again, there are splendid views – of one of the Trafalgar waterfalls and the village of Wotten Waven across the valley from this peaceful corner. The trail then moves into a section of secondary forest (trees that grow where the

Fougere. Pineapple. Jackfruit. Dianthus. Eggplant

original virgin forest has been cleared), the ground carpeted with ferns, before emerging in to a section of sun-loving flowering shrubs, such as ixora, allamanda and azalea (the latter does well at this higher, cooler altitude). Here, too, is a nursery of house-plants, which, if you live in temperate zones you will have to nurse on an indoor window-sill in a heated room. At D`Auchamps, they flourish in the natural luxuriance of sun and rain.

What to look out for A wide variety of tropical trees, fruits, flowers and vegetables along a series of trails on an old estate. A tour takes approximately one and a quarter hours with a guide. Or you can wander along the trails by yourself and relax or picnic on the benches at the viewing spots. Fee for the garden tour, plus a juice, is US$6; entry only, US$2. Open daily 9.00am to 4.00pm. A map and a list of plants is available in English and German. Accommodation in cottages.

How to get there Coming from Roseau, look for the signpost on the left-hand side of the road before Trafalgar. Telephone: 44-83346

Randy Aaron's peppers, Morne Prosper

This former sugar estate on the tip of a ridge in the lofty village of Morne Prosper is owned and worked by Randy Aaron, whose grandfather bought the Mondesire estate when it was in limes; even earlier, it had been a sugar estate. You can still see the residual stone ruins of the workings as well as a teche, an enormous copper pan used for boiling the cane. At 1300ft, this 24-acre estate is on an open location – with glorious views of Roseau below and to rainforested ridges to the north and south. Its sandy, loam soil is free draining and, despite the heavy rainfall, dries off fast. 'Any seed that drops in Morne Prosper does well,' says Randy, who remembers spending his holidays as a child at Mondesire helping his grandfather to pick limes.

The estate, employing five people full-time, is now concentrating on growing hot peppers, a crop which is showing potential for export as the world market in peppers has suddenly and dramatically expanded. Randy says he changes his emphasis from time to time because he enjoys the challenge of trying new crops. He was a pioneer in the production of passionfruit, herbs and pineapples in Dominica, and was also one of the first farmers to use a shadehouse. Randy sup-

Annatto. Epidendrum Ciliare. Sweet Potato. Ackee

plies other farmers with pepper seedlings from his shadehouse, which protects from the rain and provides a 70 per cent shade cover. At present, he is concentrating on two varieties, West Indian Red and Ma Jacques, and hopes for a yield of 20,000lbs per acre.

'I can't supply enough pepper seedlings to the farmers,' he said. 'The seedlings are 6-7 weeks old and then it's three months to the first crop. Peppers are less work than bananas and, unlike bananas, the plants can be cut back and then they rejuvenate to produce another crop.' Apart from peppers, sometimes intercropped with tomatoes or cabbages, Randy grows lettuce, chives, celery and thyme, also by multiple-cropping. The only fertiliser used is chicken manure, which is spread on the raised beds before planting out. On his north-west slopes, Randy has found that lettuces are ready to harvest within a month. For the moment, though, the hills of Morne Prosper are burgeoning with green bushes and the bright red of hot peppers.

What to look out for Hot peppers, lettuce, celery, herbs.

How to get there From Roseau, take the Wotten Waven road and after the small bridge, turn first right and climb hard until you reach Morne Prosper. Telephone: 44-98630.

Vilma Ghita's market garden

This small two-acre plot of vegetables and fruits is intensively cultivated by Vilma Ghita. It lies in a dip beside the road leading to the village of Trafalgar on one side and bounded by a ravine on the other. Vilma's well-tended garden, surrounding a family home, is typical of how the small farmers of Dominica (many of them women) work the land and provide for themselves and their families.

Everywhere you look, something is growing in the rich reddish-brown soil. Vilma knows that whatever she sows will grow well and that she will be able to sell it on her weekly visit to the Saturday market in Roseau. She grows a wide range of ground provisions – sweet potato, cush-cush, ladies' yam and dasheen. Then there is sweetcorn, a little sugar cane, pigeon peas, spinach, some pawpaw trees, and plantains and pineapples near the house. She also cultivates newer crops, introduced to Dominica more recently, such as sugar peas, string beans, watermelon. As in all smallholdings, Vilma has fruit trees, mainly for domestic use – tangerine, orange, grapefruit.

Pomerac. Silk Cotton Tree. Torch Lily. Sapodilla

Vilma plants by the moon. Crops that bear above ground are planted when the moon is going up; and crops that bear below ground, such as root vegetables, are planted when the moon is going down. Weeding is also done when the moon is going down. According to Dominican farmers, this traditional method produces better yields.

Crops that grow from seed are sown in trays rather than sown straight into the ground and then thinned out. Seedlings are pricked out into individual pots and then planted up into neat, cleanly weeded and built-up beds. Root crops are planted as a slip, or a piece of vine is broken off and tucked into the soil to grow again. Vilma uses manure from her chickens, goats and cow and feeds her animals from the weedings of the garden. It is a cyclical process. Her tools are a cutlass and a fork. As one Dominican said: 'The cutlass is the pen of the farmer.'

In its idyllic setting, it is a garden of both charm and industry, and one example of how Dominica's many smallholders contribute to the island's agricultural base.

What to look out for Vegetables and fruit grown by traditional methods

How to get there From Roseau, on the road to Trafalgar, shortly after the junction to Laudat and before the sharp bend. The house is on the right, set back from the road hidden behind a hedge of yellow crotons. Telephone: 44-80428

Much of the produce sold in Roseau market
is grown by farmers from Giraudel

GIRAUDEL VILLAGE

The villages of Giraudel and its neighbour, Eggleston, are famous in Dominica for their flowers and for their market produce. They host an annual flower show, organised by the local horticultural society. During the first weekend in May, thousands of Dominicans visit the villages to buy from the plant stalls that line the road and to admire the magnificent themed displays entered for the popular flower-arranging competition.

Giraudel lies beyond Eggleston, high up on a balmy ridge south of Roseau, where it is protected from the winds. It has marvellously open vistas down to the sea and across sweeps of mountain ridges, while to the south-east lies the peak of Morne Anglais. To be there is to be – and to feel – on top of the world.

Ma Delphine Chasseau

In front of Ma Chasseau's home is a display of cottage-garden flowers that people who garden in temperate countries could perhaps achieve for one week a year. At Giraudel, she enjoys a year-round spectacular of zinnias and dahlias, yellow day lilies, leggy pink roses, a burst of red amaryllis here, the odd chrysanthemum there, clouds of pink and mauve impatiens at the base of an old mango tree. She also cherishes a mangosteen tree that survived the destruction of Hurricane David and is still bearing fruit.

Ma Chasseau takes her produce to market every Saturday – like her neighbours from Giraudel she has a stall in the indoor section of the market. In her vegetable garden, Ma Chasseau concentrates on some of the crops introduced by the Taiwanese into Dominica in the 1980s. Below the road that crosses her land are healthy patches of broccoli and cabbage, while closer to the house she grows Chinese leeks, celery and parsley, which will be tied up with 'banana rope' into neat little bundles for the market.

Sometimes the rain will damage the young broccoli heads, but for the most part the land dries off quickly, helped by the sun and the porous nature of the soil. In her shade house, Ma Chasseau grows hybrid anthuriums from Holland, which need extra protection from

Passion Flower. Tangerine. Poui. Man Better Man

both the sun and the rain. She uses coconut husks as planting material to encourage her favourite varieties – unusual colours, such as a dark red-black and a shell pink. In another outhouse, she keeps rabbits, guineapigs, the indigenous agouti (which itself looks rather like a large guineapig) and goats.

Ma Marion Bell

Ma Bell works her lovely piece of land above the old Giraudel village graveyard from dawn to dusk, and well into the night when she is preparing for Saturday market. Now in her late sixties, she has provided for her grown family and continues to work the land single-handed.

The site is breezy and open, with sparkling views down to the sea and to the forested ridges to the north. Below her house is a magnificent field of blue agapanthus (most conspicuous in May and June). Ma Bell cuts the enormous flowerheads to make bouquets mixed with red and pink amaryllis (with four or five trumpet-shaped blooms per stalk). Or she might add sprays of the pale mauve Michaelmas daisy, maidenhair fern or a stem or two of some jaunty yellow day lilies.

She also has her citrus trees and vegetables, including beds of the increasingly popular Irish potato (as opposed to sweet potato), and herbs, used both for cooking and as bush medicine. Around the house are herbs grown for teas, such as anise (in the fennel family) and wormwood (*Ambrosia hispida*). She likes her bush teas, as she says, 'very strong'.

Rose and Glennis Nelson

The Nelson's farm is higher up the Giraudel heights than most, where the breeze is breezier and the views even more dramatic. Facing west on a gentle slope, this impressive 2.6-acre market-garden site was forest when the Nelsons bought it in the mid 1980s. They cleared the rich volcanic soil themselves, and since then they have enriched it still further with 'pen' manure (plus a little fertiliser) from their own animals. Rotating their plantings between above and below ground crops, they concentrate on celery, parsley and pepper, lettuce and turnip. In the greenhouse, further plantings of lettuce, celery and

Canna Generalis. Papaya. Cashew. Acalpha Hispida

peppers, already pricked out from the seed trays, are continually 'in production', irrigated by twice daily watering. In another protected area, Rose is also growing anthurium in tissue culture, where the plants never touch soil and the roots are enmeshed in coconut husk fibre. Rose has taken agricultural courses in Martinique and Canada and has learned about organic farming from her neighbour Andrew Royer (see below). Like other younger farmers in Dominica, Rose mixes traditional practices and traditional crops with modern methods and new crops. She sells much of her produce to local hotels and restaurants, and if you see her in the market on Saturday morning, she will be looking happy and will say that she sold everything by 7.30am.

Andrew Royer, organic farmer

Andrew Royer is proud to have been described as a 'pioneer and authority on organic farming' at a recent regional conference on 'integrated rural development'. He bought his farm, which he calls Anronat, at Giraudel his home village, in 1969. At that time the land was covered with grapefruit trees and bananas, but Andrew Royer turned to organic practices soon after because, as he says, 'I had no money for chemical inputs'. Since then, 1.1 acres of south-facing land has produced enough for him and his wife to live off and to raise six children. On a slope, which ranges in steepness from 40-80 degrees, he farms on good volcanic soil, which receives 160 inches of rain per annum.

He believes that food sustainability can be achieved only through organic methods. 'You are depleting the world's food by using chemicals; the soil loses its humus. Look what has happened in the US dust bowl,' he says.

He introduced organic practices gradually, firstly by buying a donkey and a cow and planting grasses to feed his animals. Then he decided to diversify and to cut down most of his bananas ('neighbouring farmers considered me mad') to grow not just two crops but at least 30 different ones. He levelled and terraced the land for rotating crops such as carrots, while he grew permanent crops, such as tannia, on the slopes.

Mr Royer uses interplanting, crop rotation and field sanitation for insect control because he believes that although some insects are harmful, 'man is more destructive'. He uses his weeds for his chickens

Euphorbia Splendens. Basilic. Avocado. Pigeon Pea

to scratch through and so, in a cyclical process, eventually to be returned to the earth enriched.

At one time, Mr Royer took 42 crops to market – all cultivated on his land. He says that he supplies his home, the market, and his animals. He grows only small quantities in one place, in succession planting, preferring to scatter his crops so that he can always be harvesting something at some time. And he grows cherry trees and sugar cane for his children instead of sweets.

On the steep slopes above Mr Royer's house are the animals' pens. His pigs supply the waste, which he turns into methane gas in a cylinder that feeds a pipe, which carries the gas to his house where he cooks the food from the riches of his garden. It's a cycle of inter-dependence on a Dominican hillside.

Over the years, hundreds of students, farmers and tourists from all over the world have visited Andrew Royer's farm to learn from his farming methods, and see that his small patch of land, organically farmed and efficiently managed, can provide for the needs of a family. 'Grow what you eat, eat what you grow, and sell the surplus': that is Andrew Royer's message.

What to look out for Successful market gardens growing a wide range of vegetables for local use. Colourful flower gardens.

How to get there Take the road south out of Roseau, turn left at Fortune, keep climbing until you reach Eggleston, continue to Giraudel and ask for directions. The farmer-gardeners will be happy to greet you at reasonable times of day. On Saturday mornings they are at Roseau market. Telephone: Andrew Royer: 44-83102.

CARIB TERRITORY

As the surviving indigenous people of Dominica, the Caribs, who now occupy their own Territory on the north-east coast, were the first to cultivate the land and create a 'jardin caribe' out of the 'the high woods'. And the fruits and vegetables that they used remain – for the most part – the essential ingredients of today's Dominican garden. Although they were first and foremost fine fishermen, the Caribs (who called themselves Kalinago) grew manioc, maize, beans, tobacco, sweet potatoes, peppers, pineapples, and tended fruit trees such as papaya, *kashima* (sweetsop) and *kowosol* (soursop).

The earliest European sailors used Dominica as a 'lay-by' on their journey under sail from the Canaries to the New World for, thanks to the north-east trade winds, it was their first landfall. In Dominica the new arrivals rested and took on water. They were brought fruit, including pineapples, by the Caribs. One French captain noted that some of his 'more indiscreete' sailors had 'gathered their Ananas [pineapples] in the Indians gardens, trampling through them without any discretion....' Again, in 1595, 'They [Caribs] came thither to fetch some fruits which they sowe and plant in divers places of that Island, which they keepe like gardens', said the chronicler who accompanied Drake and Hawkins on their final voyage. Then, as now, Carib gardens were some way from their dwellings.

Other practices illustrate a similar continuity in tradition. Slash and burn methods, for example, were observed in the 16th century and again in the 19th, as in this account by Frederick Ober, an American naturalist: 'Though each family has a little garden adjacent to the dwelling, any individual can select an unoccupied piece of ground on the neighboring hills, or mountain sides, for cultivation. All their provision grounds (as are called the mountain gardens where the

Simen Contra. Guava. Heliconia. Mal Estomac. Iris

staple fruit and vegetables are grown) are at a distance from the house, some even two miles way, solitary openings made in the depths of the high woods. As the soil in general is very thin, and does not support a crop for many successive years, these gardens are constantly made afresh.' This practice remains part of Carib culture (as well as being standard Dominican practice), while Carib farmers still walk long distances through the hills of the Carib Territory to cultivate their personal plots. The 'jardin caribe' has survived.

Down the centuries, manioc has been the Caribs' most important crop. It was not just eaten, it was central to Carib myths and to religious imagery. Father Raymond Breton, a French missionary stationed in Guadeloupe, arrived in Dominica in 1642 and from his account of everyday life among the Caribs, a masterful piece of social anthropology, we can learn more of the cultivation practices of the Caribs. He, too, reported that the Caribs had their 'gardens' separate from their houses; adding that the Carib women would go to their gardens 'to dig sweet potatoes or manioc...After they have uprooted the crop they clean the soil and replant the manioc or potatoes. They do not use spades, nor hoes, because they are not accustomed to them, but use a sharp stick. They dig the soil with it and make a ditch for manioc, then go back loaded with their full carrying basket.'

Breton noted how the manioc was eaten: one variety was eaten as a root vegetable, the others made into flour (farine) and then bread (cassava), and also processed into an alcoholic drink. These ways continue today (although much less so and rarely as a drink). A more recent manioc-based dumpling, with spices and sugar wrapped in a leaf, is called 'kangki', a word borrowed from Afro-Dominicans.

Breton was much taken by the sweet potato, which he called 'the mana of these islands, and having it one cannot die of hunger.' He talked about sugar cane and bananas that had been brought in by the Spanish (Europeans also introduced the Caribs to breadfruit, cocoa, coffee, mango and plantain). There was also, said Breton, a small indigenous pineapple 'which furnishes hemp for the Caribs', and types of cabbage, one of which 'was added to their cooking instead of seasoning, and their tips prepared like Spanish chard'.

Tobacco, one of the crops the Europeans noticed growing in the Caribbean, was also observed by Father Breton. Early on, the Caribs had established a tobacco trade with the French. And, even today, an elderly Carib may grow tobacco beside the house, ultimately to dry for

Mangosteen. Sweetsop. Coleus. Cassia Alata. Pilea

smoking in a pipe. The use of flowering plants in Carib yards, such as in the distinctive white flower of the tobacco plant, might first have been purely functional. But by the 1940s, the American botanist W.H. Hodge wrote that he found ornamental plants in Carib yards 'among all these economically useful species.' He reported that the chenille plant, euphorbia, hibiscus, croton and billbergia all flourished. This proved, he said somewhat loftily, 'that the Island Carib, like any other human, enjoys beauty for beauty's sake.'

As you travel through the Territory, through the scattered villages with their great backdrops of mountain and sea, the distinctiveness of Carib garden design becomes clear. The red earth is swept bare around the dwelling-houses so that the bright flowers and shrubs – hedges of crotons, dracaena and aralia, or islands of hot pepper – stand out to even greater effect. Sometimes, the little houses are surrounded by a mossy-looking grass (*zoysia*), which itself provides a cosy carpet for the brightly-flowering plants that dot Carib yards from Atkinson to Sineku.

However, much of the ornamental planting around the homes in the Carib Territory has been partly borrowed from other traditions. As the Carib people have become a little wealthier, they have brought different varieties of shrubs from other parts of Dominica – and other parts of the world – into their villages along the rugged length of the Carib Territory.

The hot colours of the canna lily also give a distinctive character to the Carib Territory. These dramatic gladioli-looking plants have long been associated with gardens in this part of Dominica. The garden of Clamence Frederick, the mother of the Carib Chief Hilary Frederick, is, for example, full of them. Her garden, surrounding a small bar at Salybia, has fine specimens of pink, yellow and red cannas mixed with begonias (*L'oseille* in Creole) and roses – a delicate pink floribunda and a pale yellow shrub rose.

The front hedge of Mrs Frederick's garden is now planted with the familiar yellow and red leafed croton. (This has replaced a diseased hibiscus hedge.) But roses remain Mrs Frederick's favourite flowers: 'When you see the flower, just one makes a bouquet,' she says, with feeling.

Ornamental flowers, most of which are to be found all over Dominica, have, however, eased out some of the traditional plants found on the edges of Carib yards. In 1942, W.H. Hodge found numerous culti-

Allamanda. Coco Chat. Arrowroot. Cactus. Vervaine

vated species growing 'for one household purpose or another'. For example, there was cotton for stuffing pillows and mattresses, and the indigenous roucou (*Bixa orellana*), whose 'bright red seeds are used as a source of colouring, but were formerly mixed with carapa oil to make a body paint and insect repellent', castor bean plants, arrowroot, calabash and the pineapple-like La Pite, 'source of a strong twine and fishing line'. Breton had observed such plants 300 years earlier. Today, none of these are common – except the castor oil plant and the calabash – although Caribs, who are conscious of what can be lost, are reclaiming the legacies handed down from their ancestors.

Kent Auguiste is a leading Carib and has been a member of the Carib Council for many years. He works as a farmer but he has also begun to plant the garden around his house in Bataka to reflect his Carib ancestry. 'Of course, I have to have gommier, I'm a Carib,' he said, pointing out a sapling gommier growing in a small ravine. The gommier (*Dacryodes excelsa*), the dominant timber species in Dominica, is traditionally associated with the Caribs who still use this fine rainforest species, as they have done for centuries, to build canoes. Now, it is under threat from over-cutting and, for Kent Auguiste, who is working hard on researching Carib history, planting a gommier is an expression of his commitment to conservation.

Much of the Carib Territory is devoted to bananas and coconuts, but Kent Auguiste left bananas behind many years ago. His land was far away and, as a conservationist, he didn't believe that bananas protected the land well. Instead, he has concentrated on passionfruit and peppers. 'I sent all my children to secondary school on passionfruit and peppers,' he said.

Beside his house, Kent Auguiste has also planted some of the shrubs and herbs used by the Caribs for ritual baths or for medicinal use. For example, there is Man better man (*Achyranthes indica*): 'It makes you move like a lion,' he said, of this herb whose leaves are used in teas – for fevers, colds, chest pains and as a tonic for tired blood. There is also kudjuruk *(Petiveria alliacea)*, traditionally used to keep bad spirits away, while the seeds of the male Canna lily (*Canna indica*), also called *Tous les mois,* are taken for stomach ache. The Caribs, says Kent Auguiste, only used odd numbers of leaves or plants in their rituals.

Auguiste also grows larouma (*Ischnosiphon arouma*), the special reed which the Caribs still use to make their excellent waterproof bas-

Asparagus. Prickly Pear. Potato Vine. Zinnia. Sage

kets. Auguiste has some larouma by his house, but he says that it grows better on the shady forest floor where it also protects the soil. The forests have been affected by clearance so that Caribs have to walk even further into the mountains for supplies of larouma.

Masterlyn Eustache is another Carib farmer; he has an acre and a half of sloping land on Horseback Ridge, with dramatic views down to the Concord River and across to the forests and mountains on one side and to the wild coastline on the other. He has been working this land since he was a small boy and the land was goat pasture. Nowadays, he grows a little sugar cane, trenches of ginger, and the castor oil plant. The latter was traditionally used by the Caribs, mixed with the red dye of the roucou, for body paint. It is still used to improve hair colour and quality. Masterlyn also retains a section of his land for manioc in much the way his ancestors would have done when they made their 'jardin caribe'.

What to look out for Flower and shrub planting around village homes; traditional craft with its links to ancient Carib agriculture and production; ask to be shown herbs and manioc.

How to get there The road threads through the villages of the Carib Territory from Castle Bruce in the south to Marigot in the north.

Floral Gardens, Concord

Floral Gardens is an appropriate name for the guesthouse at the village of Concord, which fringes the Pagua River. Not only is its garden festooned with blossoms, but as you approach the guesthouse from the coast, the road is clothed on both sides by swathes of sharply coloured crotons of every shape and texture. The garden is the creation of the owners of Floral Gardens, Lily and Oliver Seraphin, who bought an old sugar estate and began to develop the garden from bush and build their guesthouse at the start of the 1990s.

The main garden, behind the guesthouse, is on a small piece of flat land with a hillside rising steeply behind it. The garden is a maze of pathways and planting: of shrubs and fruit trees and indigenous ferns. One of the most characteristic and charming aspects of the garden lies in the variety of containers used to protect and enhance the planting. Rose bushes and a salmon pink mussaenda, which used to sit snugly in recycled car tyres as protection for the young plants, are now estab-

Pandanus. Dumb Cane. Epidendrum Discoidale. Ivy

lished. White-painted rocks, pots and conch shells provide sanctuaries for heliconias and torch gingers, hibiscus and pride of Barbados. There is even the chassis of an old car (that dates from the days before the Seraphins were married), which is now filled with the tightly packed leaves of the purple Ti plant (*Cordyline terminalis var.*). As Oliver Seraphin says: 'All these containers have their history'.

The Seraphins wanted to bring together in one place as many varieties of the plants of Dominica that they could find. Only cacti appear to have thwarted their efforts – the wet conditions were not to their liking. The Seraphins collected from friends and nurseries and tried to find rare and interesting plants, such as the red heliconia and the star apple (*Chrysophyllum cainito*). The garden is not yet mature, but its design and character is well established reflecting its owners' interests and dedication.

They are also encouraging their village neighbours in Concord to continue the shrub planting along the roadside so as to make the route through the village one long avenue of colour. It is an educational process because the villagers are accustomed to thinking that ornamentals have no economic value, said Oliver Seraphin. But the Seraphins think that the villagers could begin to sell plants to visitors, thus bringing decoration and economy together in one process.

What to look out for Wide selection of shrubs, fruit trees and local forest plants in a pleasant garden setting,. Accommodation and restaurant also available.

How to get there Go to the village of Concord, a few miles before Hatton Garden on the road from Pont Casse. Telephone: 44-57636

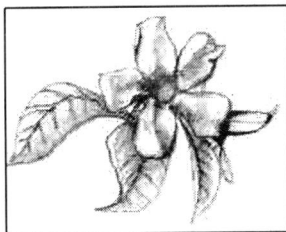

THE SOUTH

The south and south-east of Dominica have their own special atmospheres. The two villages of Pichelin and Grand Bay, for example, are known as centres for veti-ver (*Vetiveria zizanioides*), a grass used to make mats; hats are usually made out of a skrewpine (*pandanus utilis*). The veti-ver grows in clumps, thinner and finer than lemon grass. The cut grass is laid across the road edges to dry (driving over it helps flatten it). Clumps are grown on the roadside or on edges of vegetable patches. Propagated by division, it is a cut-and-come-again plant, which is taken back to its roots at harvest time.

There is a fine strip of veti-ver at the Grand Bay Agricultural Station, where it is sold in large bundles to local women who buy it to plait in to a large ball which is sold by the pound to make into intricately designed mats. It is also used as mulch to keep weeds down and as an agent for erosion control. The Agricultural Station is on nine acres of land sloping towards the sea. It is one of seven agricultural stations in Dominica whose purpose is to demonstrate good practice to farmers, to encourage diversification of crops and to distribute plants, either free of charge or for a small fee. The Agricultural Station at Grand Bay also has a herd of black-bellied sheep.

Bay trees of Petite Savanne

The sweet smell of the crushed leaves of the bay tree (*Pimenta racemosa)* or, in Creole, *bwa danne*, is everywhere in the east and south-east parts of the island, in particular around the village of Petite Savanne. The leaf of the bay is used to make bay oil, a valuable oil used in limited quantities in the perfume trade. The bay tree (it has three varieties – cinnamon, citron and clove) is a native of the West

Tomato. Alpinia Purpurata. Ixora. Pomme de Liane

Indies and grows on drier hillsides. It was one of the first spices recorded in the New World. Chanca, the surgeon on Columbus' second voyage, wrote of Marie Galante (within sight of Dominica): 'We found there a tree whose leaf had the finest smell of cloves that I have ever met with; it was in shape like a laurel leaf, but not so large.'

A small, grey-brown tree, its angular, rocket-shaped branches are harvested twice a year. The branches are broken off by hand before being dried and dispatched to small distilleries, tucked away in ravines around Petite Savanne (and east coast villages). The distilleries, which use traditional technology, will often welcome visitors. You can buy Dominica's bay rum, good for the hair and skin, in Roseau.

New Florida Estate, Bellevue Chopin

In the cool breeziness of the New Florida estate, near the village of Bellevue Chopin, you feel that perhaps you are not in the Caribbean at all, for here dark pine trees are planted among the indigenous forest. Agriculturist and estate owner, Charlie Winston, began to plant pines in the 1950s because of his 'childish love of Christmas trees'; nowadays, it is his sons, who mainly work the estate. They grow and sell Christmas trees (junipers) trying to meet a growing local demand.

Originally, there was sugar and then citrus on the land. When Charlie Winston bought it, he named it New Florida after the mass of green and gold oranges he found growing there. The pines, now grown to maturity, are Mediterranean varieties such as cuypressus, which can survive in the tropics. The first seeds were grown from a packet sent to Mr Winston from a friend in Rome. Now there are resinous glades of pine, the forest floor layered in needles and scattered with cones. The cool forest is also used for horse riding.

As well as pines, this high-altitude, shady spot is home to many varieties of African violets, grown by Melanie Winston, one of Mr Winston's daughters-in-law. Their natural habitats are the cool, almost sunless, rock-faces of east Africa. Melanie sells the violets as houseplants, and keeps them in pots under a shady porch although she has successfully planted some out under a canopy of impatiens.

What to look out for Pines and African violets .

How to get there After Bellevue Chopin, on the road to Grand Bay take the second turning on the left. Telephone: 44-82896

Traveller's Palm. Breadfruit. Celery. Passionfruit

Petit Coulibri Estate, Soufriere

At the end of a long, meadow-filled valley leading from the village of Soufriere, with its remnants of an old lime plantation, lies this wild estate bounded by mountains and the sea. The approach is through an avenue of coconut and Royal palms, opening on to a great vista of flat land backed by forest. A former sugar estate and, more recently, an aloe farm, it has been worked by Erica and Tony Burnett-Biscombe since 1994. They are the owners of La Robe Creole Restaurant in Roseau, and also of Irie Itals, a company producing plantain, dasheen and banana chips.

At present only 10 acres are under cultivation, but they are hoping to use as many of their 130 cultivatable acres as possible. There are neatly planted rows of plantains, of up to 1000 tissue-cultured plants, and fields of dasheen, used to make the chips which have already found a market in neighbouring Caribbean islands. Bananas and mangoes are made into chutneys. The estate also supplies La Robe Creole with fruit, such as pineapples and watermelon, vegetables and seasonings.

This is a hot, dry corner of Dominica with no water supply, so in the dry season water has to be brought in to irrigate the Irish potatoes, strawberries and tomatoes. In some months of the year, it is also too hot and dry for such crops as lettuce and cabbage. At this time, weeds are left in place to retain shade and moisture. To help control the wind, more windbreaks of productive fruit trees, such as cherry, soursop and ackee, will be planted to augment the existing windbreaks of galba and mango. At 600ft altitude, there is sometimes dew in the morning.

The Burnett-Biscombes are planning both to bring the 'chip' processing plant to the estate and also to live there. An old house, built on the site of the original estate, faces a lawn, with flowering shrubs and the ruins of a cattle-mill, one of the few such relics on the island.

What to look out for Vegetables, fruits, bananas and plantain in a wonderful open setting.

How to get there From Soufriere, take the road towards the sulphur springs, then turn right and follow the signs to the junction between Petit Coulibri cottages and Petit Coulibri estate. Telephone: 44-82896

Jasmine. Mussaenda. Christophene. Custard Apple

Bananas are Dominica's main export crop. Vital to the economy, they are grown all over the island

IN OTHER CORNERS

Wherever you look in Dominica, there is evidence of land under cultivation. And each village has a particular personality deriving from the nature of its environment and the history of its people. The coastal villages in the north, such as Calibishie, for example, are particularly pretty, with their flowering hedges of bright-red hibiscus garlanding wooden homes, while, during the months around Christmas, gardens in the eastern villages of La Plaine and Delices are smothered in the scarlet bracts of tree-sized poinsettias. Remote communities in the east, such as Petite Soufriere, cultivate bay trees among the coconut, mango and banana.

The large sugar estates in the east, such as those at Castle Bruce and Rosalie, are no more – the only evidence of their existence is the geographical spread of the villages, away from the best lands in the valley, and the ruins, for example, of the aqueduct at Rosalie. However, there are still large estates – of coconuts – around Hampstead and Blenheim, in the north. And, as this chapter shows, Dominica has yet more cultivated corners to explore.

Newfoundland Flowers, Rosalie

By Dominican standards, Dennis Labassiere has a large estate, of more than 300 wild acres hidden away off the road approaching Rosalie, on the east coast. There is a sense of surprise when a winding track opens up into a dramatic basin, criss-crossed by five rushing rivers, including the Rosalie River itself, and backed by mountains. Labassiere bought the estate in the early 1990s, and he is concentrating on bananas, plantains and, more recently, anthurium.

On the flat area close to the estate house, he has three acres of greenhouses planted with anthurium. This makes him by far the largest producer of anthurium in Dominica: 'No one else is doing it so commercially,' he says. He is growing 26 tissue-cultured anthurium varieties. Grown on coconut husks and protected from the sun and the rain, these hybrids from Hawaii and Holland have colours of great subtlety, from pastel greens splashed with pink, to white and a deep purple. The flowers from his 20,000 plants will be exported through neighbouring Martinique to Europe. Wholesalers in Martinique are

Kudjuruk. Ginger. Poinsettia. Plantain. Lime. Clove

keen to buy from Dominica where the costs of production are lower.

Away from the anthurium shadehouses, Labassiere has 25 acres of land under bananas. These rich acres on the valley floor produce 300 boxes (each one of 33lbs) of bananas a week, in contrast to the smaller volumes produced by most Dominican farmers. Larger farmers like Labassiere, who can produce volume and top quality fruit, still find it profitable to grow bananas. Anthuriums, however, are one way of diversifying out of a dependency on one crop. Labassiere also plans to introduce coconut and ruby grapefruit on the lower slopes of his land. His estate is an example of how a modern Dominican 'planter' can develop his garden.

What to look out for Hybrid anthuriums for export; intensive banana production

How to get there From Roseau, take the road for Rosalie. After the Emerald Pool turn-off, continue past the boxing plant on the right and a long row of coconut palms, then look out for a sign for Newfoundland Flowers.

Father Maupetit, Vielle Case

Fruit and nut trees grace the garden of the presbytery perched above Vielle Case, the northern village where, in 1642, the French-born Father Breton said the first mass in Dominica in the carbet of the local Carib chief. Three hundred and fifty years later, Father Hilaire Maupetit is the village priest. He is also a Frenchman, brought up on a farm in the west of France. He has lived in Vielle Case – with its lovely simple church – since 1973, and has created his garden from what was a small kitchen garden and a paddock for sheep and goats.

Over the years, a fence was put up round the four-acre property, old mango trees were cut and a lawn created. Father Maupetit was brought seeds of unusual fruit trees, palms and countless other plants. He propagated these and planted them out in rows running parallel to the south-facing slope that runs down to a dry wall. This wonderful, open 'forest garden' has a European feel, with its bearing trees, a kitchen garden of lettuce, radish, okra and pepper, flowering plants at its borders, and a black pepper vine crawling up the back wall of the presbytery. Father Maupetit's eyes sparkle with joy at being able to offer his visitors freshly picked, rare fruits warmed by the sun. A

Anise. Plumbago Capensis. Spider Lily. Anthurium

super-sweet carambola, perhaps, or a hybrid guava. He loves all his trees and plants, but if he had to choose a special one, it would be, he said, the paradise nut tree which produces an enormous pod rather like a flower pot.

His life is full: getting up at 4.20am to pray and read psalms, and preaching every day in different villages. There are also his bees to raise and a dark and richly-flavoured honey to make, as well as hard work in the garden. For Father Maupetit the joy is in growing things. The complexity of each plant shows divine creation, he says, for 'No man could have conceived all this.'

What to look out for Rare fruit and nut trees, a palm collection and kitchen garden

How to get there Take the turning towards Pennville off the Portsmouth-Marigot road. Continue to Vielle Case, turn left past the police station, up to the church and presbytery. Telephone: 44-55570

Growing bananas

Wilson Ismael is one of hundreds of small farmers who, up to the late 1990s, depended on growing bananas to feed their families, send their children to school and pay their mortgages. Ismael lives in Mahaut, a large coastal village north of Roseau, but his 4.5 acres of land that he inherited from his family, lies on the slopes of the Layou valley, some five miles from Mahaut. Bananas can be grown on most soils from sea level to the mountains, although a deep loam, well-drained soil is best. Ismael says that his soil is rich although his land is relatively steep.

Propagation of bananas is from suckers, which spring up from the sides of the plant. Bananas need constant attention and take nine months to mature, which are two reasons why Dominican farmers will say that 'a banana is like a baby'. Nowadays, bananas are given doses of herbicides and pesticides, while the ripening fruit is covered with a blue plastic bag to protect it from bugs and birds so that the skin looks flawless for the demanding consumer. In the past, says Wilson Ismael, there was less emphasis on the maintenance of the plant and the preparation of the fruit. Now, farmers are urged to use pesticides (some of which are now banned in the United Kingdom and the United States). Wilson Ismael says that chemicals help get rid of pests

Breadfruit. Pomegranate. Cucumber. Sugar Cane

but the disadvantages are in the after effects: retarded growth, a difference in taste, and problems in repeat planting.

The commercial production of bananas for export began in Dominica in the 1930s, but it was not until the 1950s that regular shipments were made to Britain. Since then, the Dominican economy has become dependent on the banana, producing a record EC$104m, for example, in 1988. For many decades, the British company Geest controlled the shipping and marketing of Dominican bananas (along with those from the other Windward Islands).

In 1996, Geest sold its interests to a new company made up of the four Windward Island governments and the Irish fruit company, Fyffes. The new company continued to ship and market Caribbean bananas to Britain under its agreement with the European Union which gave preference, under a quota and licensing system, to Caribbean bananas. So Caribbean farmers could still rely on a regular income from the sale of their bananas. This banana wealth, known as 'green gold', became a vital component of the Dominican economy, giving many Dominicans an opportunity to participate in a cash economy for the first time, and even to save money.

Every week, the pick-up trucks, loaded high with bananas, queue up to unload their harvest at Woodbridge Bay port. Some may wait all day and half the night, but the work has begun the night before when the farmers prepare the chemicals that are used to wash the fruit before packing. The bunches that are ready to be picked – still green but three-quarters mature – are cut from the plant and carried gently in trays to the 'field shed' where each hand is washed, weighed, packed tidily into boxes of 33lbs and taken to the banana boat. In 1997, Wilson Ismael earned EC$12-EC$13 per box for grade A fruit, EC$8 for grade B fruit and EC$6 for the lowest quality fruit. Prices have been decreasing for some time and Wilson Ismael has come to realise that bananas are not worth all the hard work, despite his pride and pleasure in 'the beauty of a well-kept field'. He says that 'banana is modern day enslavement. The overheads and the labour costs are much too high now and it is not profitable.'

What has persuaded Ismael to move away from bananas – and to concentrate more on tree crops, livestock and vegetables – is a further development, which has nothing to do with how hard he works or what sort of quality of bananas he produces. His plight, like that of every other Caribbean farmer, is being decided thousands of miles

African Tulip Tree. Cereus. Lignum Vitae. Radish

away – among the fat cats of capitalism in Chicago and the bureaucrats of Brussels.

Pressure on the Caribbean's European banana market began to increase in the early 1990s: the threat came from the larger, yellower, more plastic-looking Latin American banana, most of which are grown on vast plantations owned by North American multi-nationals such as Dole and Chiquita. The Caribbean banana grown by thousands of small independent farmers can not compete with the 'dollar' banana from Latin America, where flat land, lower labour costs and intensive methods of farming mean that more bananas can be produced for less.

Then, in 1996, Chiquita and Dole, not content with controlling two-thirds of the European market, complained to the United States that under World Trade Organisation (WTO) rules the Caribbean's agreement with Europe was unfair and protectionist. The WTO, with its philosophy of free trade, ruled in favour of the greedy giants in September 1997. The Caribbean could only complain bitterly that the United States' action would put thousands of farmers out of business and create major economic distress. Wilson Ismael, for example, is pessimistic about the future. 'The market is unsure, the price unstable', he says. He argues that 'without a sure market for other crops, farmers will be frustrated, there will be more crime, more drugs and less development.'

Wilson Ismael is not alone in his views. Every Dominican will express concern about the future of the banana industry. If you are interested, you can ask any Dominican to explain about the cultivation of the banana. And no one makes jokes about 'banana skins' or 'banana splits' in the Caribbean. Rather, the banana is part of local culture and the banana farmer is admired: as the banana farmer in the famous poem by the Jamaican Evan Jones says: 'Praise God an m'big right han/ I will live and die a banana man.'

Rainforest Mushrooms, Corona

Matthew and Christine Luke, owners of Rainforest Mushrooms, have been experimenting with mushroom growing for more than a decade, learning the best way to grow them in local conditions. The cool, wet micro-climates of the rainforests of Dominica are ideal. An indigenous species of Pleurotus, known locally as *champignon pòwyé*, grows on the stumps and logs of the white cedar tree. It is an oyster mushroom

Lantana Camara. Okra. Chaconia. Star Apple. Chive

with a large white cap, oyster-shell shaped and grows laterally in groups. Matthew learned from his grandfather to identify the edible mushrooms of the forest. The *champignon pòwyé* is eaten in a local stew made with coconut milk and called sancoche.

This gourmet oyster mushroom is cultivated organically on a substrate (growing medium) of sugar cane bagasse (pressed stalk), with added coffee husks, sawdust and crushed sea shells. This is pasteurised at 80 degrees C for four hours. When cool, the substrate is inoculated with spawn (mushroom culture) and put in trays to incubate in a dark room for 10 days. Then the trays are brought out into the light and high humidity of a greenhouse, and the mushrooms will be ready to harvest in six days. Each tray will produce four harvests (flushes) of mushrooms every 10 days until the nutrients are used up.

Rainforest Mushrooms also grow the medicinal mushroom, Reishi or Ling Chi, which is also indigenous to Dominica. They also propagate the spawn for these species, and maintain a species bank of other edible mushrooms of the region. The Lukes sell their mushrooms fresh, dried and processed (to be made into mushroom pepper sauce by the local firm, Bello). They will also distribute spawned substrate to other farmers. Growing mushrooms is a good example of sustainable agriculture co-existing with the rainforest.

What to look out for A mushroom museum, and café where you can taste local mushroom specialities and drink bush teas. Mushroom products, art, craft, incense and medicinal herbs also available.

How to get there Nine miles from Canefield up the Imperial Road, one mile south of the Pont Casse roundabout. Look for the big mushroom sign. Tel: 44-91836

Other hotels and guesthouses

All the hotels and guesthouses of Dominica take trouble to create gardens and conserve surrounding vegetation. Along with Papillote Wilderness Retreat (see page 32) and Floral Gardens (see page 47), here are some of Dominica's other hotels and guesthouses with interesting garden features.

Castaways Hotel (Telephone: 44-96244) on the west coast, was the first hotel to open in Dominica. Its dry, hot seaside position beside a sandy beach suits palms, and they are there in abundance: varieties

Cocouli. Cupid's Paint Brush. Mimosa. Selaginella

include fan, queen, royal, fishtail and a long row of pigmy date palms. Between the hotel and the road are traveller's palms and frangipani and, giving a sharp twist of colour to a roadside corner, the brilliant red florescence of the flamboyant trees. At the end of the dry season, around April/May, flowering trees all over the island explode into colour. A similar display of flamboyants can be seen against the blue of the sea, bordering the cliff-edge cemetery at the village of Massacre, to the south of Castaways.

Exotica is typical of the Giraudel area in its sunny, open position and sweet breezes. Each of the six cottages is named after a fruit (such as tamarind or soursop) and a tree of the same name grows in the front garden. Around each cottage the planting is different, but the accent is on swathes of bright colour, from hot orange marigolds to lipstick pink zinnias, and a host of other herbaceous flowers that bloom in happy profusion. Vegetables and fruit trees are grown organically. Telephone: 44-88839.

Petit Coulibri Guest Cottages (nominated by Conde Nast Traveler Magazine in 1997 as one of the world's top 25 'resorts') have spectacular views to Martinique and also inland, down a steep valley that swings back to the village of Soufriere. There are roses and Mexican flame vines around the swimming pool; a vegetable garden supplies the kitchen and the restaurant. Telephone: 44-63150.

Springfield Guesthouse, with its row of royal palms and smell of flowering citrus perfuming the air, is a converted plantation house, along the Imperial Road, about four miles above Canefield. Charlie Bellot, a local planter, originally owned much of the land, but in 1935, he sold 198 acres to John Archbold, an American millionaire, who worked the estate growing citrus, vanilla, coconut and banana. When the writer Alec Waugh visited Springfield in the late 1940s and met Archbold, he wrote: 'From its veranda you can see a narrow triangle of horizon, framed between two cliffs. The mountains rise on either side of it, high and vertical, but not so close as to make you feel shut in. In the immediate foreground is the deep gorge of a river with banana plants climbing up its sides.' Archbold, who died in 1993, transferred much of the estate to Clemson University, South Carolina, for use as a tropical research field station – while the house remains a guesthouse. Telephone: 44-91401

Zandoli Inn is a new small hotel perched on a rocky promontory at

Igname Blanche. Cauliflower. Hydrangea. Bwa Flot

Roche Cassee, close to the village of Bagatelle, on the south coast. Guests who are staying at Zandoli will enjoy the undulating trails through a mixed forest, where bay trees mingle with a rich variety of newly planted saplings, such as Surinam cherry, coconut, jacaranda, balata, pois doux. This fledgling arboretum has all been planted since 1990. There are splendid views across to the mountains of Grand Bay and, on a clear day, south to Martinique. Telephone: 44-63161.

SEE PAGE 64
FOR INFORMATION ON
GARDEN VISITS,
AND WHERE TO BUY OR ORDER THIS BOOK
(BY TELEPHONE, FAX OR EMAIL)
IN DOMINICA AND THE UK

BIBLIOGRAPHY

Allfrey, Phyllis Shand, *The Orchid House* (Virago, 1982)

Atwood, William, *The History of the Island of Dominica* (London, 1791)

Ayensu, Edward Solomon, *Medicinal Plants of the West Indies* (Reference Publications, Michigan, 1981)

Birge, William S, *In Old Roseau* (Isaac H. Blanchard, NY, 1900)

Bourne, M.J, Lennox, G.W, and Seddon, S.A, *Fruits and Vegetables of the Caribbean* (Macmillan, 1988)

Breton, Raymond, *Dictionaire Caraibe-Française* (Auxerre, 1665)

Brockway, Lucile H, *Science and Colonial Expansion: The Role of the British Royal Botanical Gardens* (Academic Press, 1979)

Buée, William Urban, *A Narrative on the Successful Manner of Cultivating the Clove Tree in the Island of Dominica* (1789)

Bulletin of Miscellaneous Information, Royal Botanic Gardens, Kew (1891, 1893,1894)

Carrington, Sean, *Wild Plants of Barbados* (Macmillan Caribbean, 1993)

Collett, Jill and Bowe, Patrick, *Caribbean Gardens* (Macmillan, 1998)

Dominica: Environmental Profile (Caribbean Conservation Association, 1991)

Dominica's Botanic Gardens, Guide to Selected Trees and Shrubs (Ministry of Agriculture, Dominica , 1988)

Edwards, Bryan, *The History Civil and Commercial of the British Colonies in the West Indies* (Dublin, 1819)

Ferguson, James, with Jason Wilson, *Traveller's Literary Companion to the Caribbean* (In Print Publishing, 1997)

Fermor, Patrick Leigh, *The Traveller's Tree* (Penguin edition, 1984)

Fraser, H et al, *A-Z of Barbadian Heritage* (Heinemann, 1990)

Froude, J.A, *The English in the West Indies* (Longmans, Green & Co, 1888)

Grimé, William, *Botany of the Black Americas* (Reference Publications, Michigan, 1976)

Grove, Richard H, *Green Imperialism* (Cambridge University Press, 1995)

Hargreaves, Dorothy and Bob, *Tropical Trees* (Hargreaves, 1960)

Harris, David R, *Plants, Animals, and Man in the Outer Leeward Islands, West Indies* (University of California Press, 1965)

Hawys, Stephen, *Mount Joy* (Duckworth, 1968)

Hodge, Walter H, *A Botanist's Dominica Diary* (The Scientific
    Monthly, March/April 1944)
—, *Flora of Dominica, British West Indies* (Lloydia,
    Volume 17, 1954)
—, *Plants Used by the Dominica Caribs* (Journal of the
    New York Botanical Garden, vol 43, August 1942)
Hodge, W.H. and Taylor, Douglas, *The Ethnobotany of the Island
    Caribs of Dominica* (Webbia 12.2, 1957)
Honychurch, Lennox, *Our Island Culture* (Letchworth Press, 1988)
—, *Dominica. Isle of Adventure* (Macmillan, 1991)
— , *The Dominica Story* (Macmillan, 1995)
— , *Carib to Creole: Contact and Culture Exchange in Dominica*
    (unpublished thesis, Bodleian Library, Oxford, 1997)
Honychurch, Penelope, *Caribbean Wild Plants and Their Uses*
    (Macmillan, 1980)
Honychurch, Penelope and Putney, A, *Geology and Soils* (Dominica
    National Park Service, 1978)
Howard, Richard A and Elizabeth S (eds), *Alexander Anderson's
    Account of The St Vincent Botanic Garden* (Cambridge,
    Mass: Harvard College, 1983)
Hoyles, Martin, *The Story of Gardening* (Journeyman Press, 1991)
Hulme, Peter and Whitehead, Neil (eds), *Wild Majesty* (Oxford
    University Press, 1992)
James, Arlington, *Cabrits Plants and their Uses* (Forestry and
    Wildlife Division, Ministry of Agriculture, 1986)
Kingsbury, John M, *Tropical Plants of the Caribbean* (Bullbrier
    Press, 1988)
Labat, J.B., *The Memoirs of Père Labat, 1693-1705* (Frank Cass,
    1970)
Lennox, G.W and Seddon, S.A., *Flowers of the Caribbean*
    (Macmillan, 1978)
Morris, D, *Report of the Economic Resources of the West Indies*
    (1898)
New Forester, The, Volume 11 (Ministry of Agriculture, 1988)
Nicholls, H.A.A, *A Text Book of Tropical Agriculture* (Macmillan,
    1897)
North, Marianne, *A Vision of Eden* (Webb & Bower, 1980)
Ober, Frank, *Camps in the Caribees* (Edinburgh, 1880)
Paravisini-Gerbert, Lizabeth, *Phyllis Shand Allfrey, A Caribbean Life*
    (Rutgers University Press, 1996)

Pattullo, Polly, *Last Resorts: the cost of tourism in the Caribbean* (*Latin America Bureau, 1996*)
Pope-Hennessy, James, *The Baths of Absalom* (Allan Wingate, 1954)
Research and Popular Uses of Medicinal Plants, report of seminar (Roseau, 1990)
Rhys, Jean, *Smile Please* (Andre Deutsch, 1979)
Sterns-Fadelle, F, *Dominica, A Fertile Isle* (Dominica, 1902)
Tussa, F.R, *Flore des Antilles*, vol 1-4 (Paris, 1808-27)
Waugh, Alex, *The Sugar Islands* (Cassell, 1958)
Webster, Aimee, *Caribbean Gardening and Flower Arranging* (Jamaica, 1968)
Winsnes, Selena Axelrod (ed), *Letters on West Africa and the Slave Trade.* Paul Erdman Isert's Journey to Guinea and the Caribbean Islands in Columbia (Oxford University Press, 1992)

USEFUL CONTACTS:

- Dominica Tourist Board, Roseau
  Telephone: 44-82045
- Dominica Conservation Association, Roseau
  Telephone: 44-84098
- Dominica Horticultural Society, PO Box 471, Roseau, Commonwealth of Dominica. The Society was founded in 1986 and has shown at exhibitions both at home and abroad. In 1995, the Society exhibited at the Chelsea Flower Show in London
- Caribbean Conservation Association, Savannah Lodge, The Garrison, St Michael, Barbados
- Caribbean Environment Watch, a quarterly magazine of news, views and reports. Inquiries: 141 Coldershaw Road, London W13 9DU, United Kingdom

GARDEN TOURS

The owners of the gardens featured in this book would be happy to show you around their garden. But please telephone first to arrange a convenient time for your visit. Alternatively, if you would like to have a tour of any – or all - of the gardens organised for you, please contact

Papillote Wilderness Retreat
Telephone: 44-82287

COPIES OF THIS BOOK ARE AVAILABLE FROM:

in DOMINICA

Papillote Wilderness Retreat, PO Box 67, Roseau, Commonwealth of Dominica, eastern Caribbean, and other outlets
Email: papillote@cwdom.dm

AND

in the UNITED KINGDOM

The Papillote Press, 23 Rozel Road, London SW4 OEY
Telephone/fax: 0171 720 5983
Email: pollyp@globalnet.co.uk